IMPROVISATION

IMPROVISATION

JOHN HODGSON
AND
ERNEST RICHARDS

Grove Press, Inc.
New York

First Published in 1966 by Methuen & Co Ltd, London, England.

First Evergreen Edition 1979
First Printing 1979
ISBN: 0-394-17099-7
Grove Press ISBN: 0-8021-4272-9
Library of Congress Catalog Card Number: 79-52093

LIBRARY OF CONGRESS CATALOGING IN PUBLICATION DATA

Hodgson, John Reed.
  Improvisation.

  Reprint of the new rev. ed. published by Eyre Methuen, London.
  Bibliography: p.
  Includes index.
  1. Improvisation (Acting) I. Richards, Ernest, joint
author. II. Title.
PN2071.I5H59 1979   792'.028   79-52093
ISBN 0-394-17099-7

Manufactured in the United States of America

Distributed by Random House, Inc., New York

GROVE PRESS, INC., 196 West Houston Street, New York, N.Y. 10014

CONTENTS

FOREWORD

I THINK MUCH OF THIS BOOK IS VERY IMPORTANT INDEED, and I hope it will be widely read. It is of the greatest importance, first of all, to *everyone* concerned with education and the lives of young people. For those interested in the theatre the very clear examination of the psychology of acting is fascinating reading.

There is a sentence in Chapter 2 which I think sums up why (without necessarily agreeing with all of it) I feel so warmly disposed towards this book: ". . . the qualities needed for the best acting are also those needed for the fullest living". This I had suspected for many years: my experience as Principal of the London Academy of Music and Dramatic Art during the last twelve years has proved it for me. We work entirely for the theatre, to give it the kind of actors and actresses it will need in the future, but doing this has led us to methods and attitudes which we can see having remarkable effects on the quality of living and being of many of our students. If more of those concerned with education took the real lessons of this book to heart, our job would be easier, and the world might be happier.

These lessons, as I interpret the book, and as my experience has shown me, are that the most important values in human life are: awareness – for want of a better word – "consciousness" is so misunderstood and misused; sensitivity; freedom; and the self-confidence that comes from the knowledge that every one of us is a unique individual, with a valuable role to play, if we can become ourselves enough to find it, and accept it. These may seem high claims to make for a book setting out to explain, in a very practical way, some methods that can be used in drama related to education, and in the education of the actor. I think they are justified by the authors' attitude to life, and to people. What they have written has grown from a happy combination of what they are, how they have learned to think and feel, and their practical experience.

Throughout the early part of the book, and explicit in the rest, runs the idea of man as a tripartite animal; consisting of body, mind, and emotion. Only when all three are functioning in harmony, and in the proper proportion for the particular job in hand, do things go right. It is this understanding that makes the book important; because this is not generally understood, or even when it is glimpsed, it is not practised.

When, after a good many years as a professional director in the London theatre, I became dissatisfied with my work, and with much that I felt around me, and decided to devote myself for a time to the problems of training, I was very clear about some things, and very ignorant about others. I knew what I sought in the theatre, and especially in acting: a particular kind of truth, freedom, a special sort of energy, arising from an awareness that lit up actors and audiences, and sent them out of the theatre feeling happier and better. I had learned that the best actors and actresses could reach this in different degrees, for different lengths of time, some most of the time, and some only in flashes. I found the younger people were often very far from it; sometimes they had glimpsed it in their early days, from the first fresh flush of their talent, but they did not understand it, and had no means of making it deeper and more permanent.

It seemed to me that, as this was something I believed to be of great value, and the birthright of those with a particular gift for the theatre, there should be methods for helping more people to grasp it more of the time. It was in search for this that I left my work as a director of plays to devote myself to training. In the process, I became intensely interested and involved in problems of education, and mostly dissatisfied with what I found. In my ignorance, I was greatly blessed in the people I found to work with: first Miss Iris Warren, who had found methods by which the right use of the voice could release the most real part of people, and make easy the manifestation of their best emotional and imaginative life: then, my colleague over these twelve years, Norman Ayrton, whose work on the body followed the principles of Iris Warren's on the voice; and who had been educated in the theatre by that great teacher Michel St Denis.

Then there was Brian Way, who although a man of the theatre had discovered a great deal from working with children. His work completed our pattern. I knew from the beginning that he brought something, the effect of which I could see clearly in the students, which I had realized was necessary, but not fully understood. It was *Improvisation*. That, at least, is what we called it, or rather *Group Improvisation* – the additional word is important. It was, in fact, the sort of thing that is described in this book: the cultivation of sensitivity, awareness, and freedom.

Michael MacOwan

London Academy of Music and
Dramatic Art

PREFACE

Improvising is as natural as talking or moving.

This book examines how this natural activity of improvising can be understood, harnessed and developed in theatre, therapy and education.

In the years since it was first published a great deal of use has been made of it in many different areas. It has found its way into schools, colleges and universities, been translated into Italian, been used as a way of teaching French and other foreign languages, and has been used by a wide range of people concerned with social awareness and rehabilitation. It has been used as a means of supplying ideas and techniques for developing a wide range of plays.

When the book was first written, the Lord Chamberlain's Office still held authoritative sway over public productions. Every word to be spoken in performance had by law to have been submitted to and been given the approving licence by the Lord Chamberlain. Now that this procedure has been abolished, both amateur and professional groups enjoy much greater freedom in making plays, and more groups are willing to try out ideas and take risks in developing their own material. Some very imaginative plays have evolved for children arising from stream-of-consciousness ideas drawn from recollections of childhood, and worked on through improvised scenes and incidents until finally a lively production has emerged. On another level, local conflicts or aspects of local history have been used as starting points for creating documentary drama. A group, for instance, working near Barnsley investigated a £4,000,000 centre development scheme designed to replace the traditional open market by car parks, shops and office blocks. In this case, the improvisation included the use of film cameras, slides, tape recorded comments from local people as well as songs, dialogue and scenes developed from the observation and experience of the actors in the locality.

Improvisation has also been used in exploring other multi-media work and in co-ordinating a wide range of ideas. In the United States, perhaps more than in Europe, there has been a proliferation of professional and amateur groups eager to take the risk of presenting entire performances on improvised material. Such groups as The Wing in San Francisco and Theatre Machine in London spontaneously present scenes or a whole play from ideas drawn from the audience or from rough scenarios supplied by the director. There are now many more fringe groups who develop productions from improvisation sessions and recent years have seen quite large prices charged for performances of what seem no more than actor-training sessions or audience involvement in encounter group activities.

In Education there has been a great resurgence of interest in game-form activities, though not always with adequate understanding. Too many teachers have used games as warm-up and introductory activities without seeing clearly enough how these games in fact worked as introductions. Sometimes game activities were justified verbally by the teacher instead of the teacher thinking out the games carefully enough so that they wouldn't need extraneous justification. There are still examples of improvisations which are pursued for self-indulgence. These tend to ramble on with a few people being lost in their fantasies and role-play without regard for the rest of the group. From time to time, we still see examples from experienced teachers which show their own confusion over aims and objectives in improvisation. With these factors in mind, we have undertaken a revision of those parts of the book where we feel further clarification is still required. The ideas, examples and suggestions still remain basic and, rather than elaborate on these in the light of our continuing experience and thinking, we have included suggestions for further reading for those who want to follow through some of the leads given through this book.

The book is divided into three sections.

Section one looks in more detail at the wide applications, the background and the values of drama improvisation. In section two, there are suggestions for ways and means of improvising starting from ideas, situations and roles which are unscripted or where the group participating are not initially using a script. Section three takes as its starting point the scripted play and suggests how improvisation can be used to discover the text and lead to an imaginative group production of it.

The chapters follow a progression because we felt the need for a sense of development and purpose in such a book. Different people, however, may wish to begin at different points. Some may wish to start straight away with the practical work, and so may find themselves turning immediately to section two or three. Nor is it envisaged that every aspect of every chapter should be exhausted before moving on. Skills like those suggested for developing concentration and imagination will be being used most of the time. Questions which we think will already be in peoples' minds have been faced. The book, we hope, will raise other questions which people wish to solve through their improvising.

For some the aim may be primarily therapeutic, for others mainly educational. Some may have largely social aims, the aims for others may be primarily artistic and creative. Some might find they want to work without a text most of the time. Others may wish to use a text or a starting point and branch out into improvisations less directly connected or wholly unconnected with the text as they proceed. Whatever method is adopted, it is hoped that this book, like the text of a play, will be seen as only the beginning and that the more receptive and responsive everyone remains, the more scope for imaginative improvisation there will be.

John Hodgson
Ernest Richards

AUTHORS' ACKNOWLEDGEMENTS

NO WORK IN DRAMA CAN BE DONE IN ISOLATION AND every time one sees improvisation or reads about drama work, there is a stimulus to one's own thinking. In this way we are indebted to many people who have worked in this field. Particularly, however, we would like to thank all the students, past and present of many different ages and backgrounds, with whom we have worked. Any discovery or creativity of ours has been stimulated by their energy, initiative and enthusiasm and even, at times, by their reluctance. Our learning has been very much in the group situation.

For work in typing the manuscript we are grateful to Mrs Kathleen Clarke and Mrs Dorothy Clark.

We are pleased to acknowledge permission to reproduce copyright material from Geoffrey Bles Ltd for an extract from Stanislavsky's *An Actor Prepares* and from Max Reinhardt Ltd for an extract from Stanislavsky's *Building a Character*.

We are also indebted to the lively theatre magazine *Encore* (now incorporated into *Plays and Players*) for extracts from two articles, "Working With Joan" (1960) and "Act of San Francisco at Edinburgh" (1963).

PART I

IMPROVISATION:

its nature and purpose

CHAPTER 1

Improvising in Life and Drama

WHAT IS IMPROVISING?

The word "improvisation" is used in so many different contexts that we had better begin by attempting to clarify what it is that this book is exploring. For some people, "improvisation" suggests no more than making do – the need only to cope somehow with blocked drains or with mending motor-cars with bootlaces on Blubberhouse Moor.

While, of course, most people are delighted by the ingenuity involved, the trouble with most of this kind of improvising is that it remains associated with the second-best and the makeshift. We never ourselves meet the challenge of thinking our way through an unexpected situation; we side-step opportunity for discovery and are merely relieved to "get by".

Another approach to improvising is, for instance, when we run up the latest fashion model from last year's cast-offs, or produce a Cordon Bleu meal from the weekend's leftovers. There is still a sense of making do, but this time we are drawing upon our imaginations in order to try and achieve an objective we have set ourselves.

There is a further aspect of improvising we meet in day-to-day living: we are continually having to adjust to whatever happens around us. The more unexpected the happening, the more spontaneous and frank the response is likely to be. Because people are less predictable than things, we are more often called upon to adjust to others in a way we cannot easily plan. If we are open and receptive, we can make discoveries both about ourselves and others from these moments. If we are less receptive, the tendency will be to reproduce what we consider to be socially acceptable responses which become standardized and stereotyped.

While drama improvisation is not the same as these examples (though indeed at times, it may be difficult to distinguish between them), it does draw upon factors inherent in them. Through situations in which we have to improvise, we can be made to draw on our own resources, to think out basic principles. We are not able to fall back on other people telling us, nor can we find instructions precise enough to cover every set of circumstances. Improvisation in drama aims to utilize the two elements from everyday life improvisation: the spontaneous response to the unfolding of an unexpected situation, and the ingenuity called on to deal with the situation; both of these in order to gain insight into problems presented.

Improvisation is a word much used these days in the discussion of drama. Sometimes improvisation is begun without the user having thought much about it, or without his knowing quite what he's doing, and sometimes those who feel it could be of use, are not sure enough about it to begin. Some people talk about it confidently and approvingly. Others speak of it more diffidently and even with suspicion. On the one side, it is seen as a vital new means of exploring the dramatic and human situation, or a way of group activity, and on the other it still has not developed much beyond its charade and party-game links.

It could be that more is said about improvisation than is known about its values and application.

BACKGROUND TO IMPROVISATION

In fact, it has a long history, as long as the history of man himself, ranging from primitive ritual to present-day "happenings". All art forms have begun with improvisation, and the early narrative epics like *The Odyssey* and *The Iliad* began as improvised storytelling. Song and dance and early dramatic ritual took more formal shape after long periods of improvisation. Improvisation has continued to be employed in comedy and in nomadic entertainment with notable periods, such as Greek and Roman comedy and Italian *commedia dell'arte* with all its influences. And today improvisation has found its way into quite a wide variety of aspects of programmes for actors, in business and vocational courses, in the training of teachers, in psychotherapy and many facets of education. Over and over again its value in one field or another has been indicated.

IN CHILDREN'S PLAY

Drama improvisation can be seen in one form by observing children playing. A four-year-old, Jayne, for instance, took a visitor on an imaginary shopping expedition, insisting that he undertake the whole ritual involved in this daily routine. Jayne took the part of Mother, her doll's pram served to convey an imaginary younger sister and the visitor seemed to find himself being a child. Together they crossed roads, avoiding traffic, went into several shops, ordered food and groceries, paid for these, and waited for change, all to a chorus of "It won't be long now," when Jayne sensed the visitor's impatience. In her play, Jayne was improvising a situation which enabled her not only to try out another role, but to transfer parts and see a very usual situation in a completely different perspective.

Fiona, at about the same age, used the transferred roles in improvised play for another purpose, it seems. She took her large teddy bear and obliged him to sit on the potty, while she played the Mother's role. It looked as though she was not only enjoying the insight gained from playing another part, but also making her own situation more bearable by distancing a ritual over which she felt some indignity. When her baby brother was being nursed one day on her mother's knee, she played another game and ran from the room. She remained outside the door, declaring, "Mummy won't let me in". By joining in this piece of improvisation, her mother was able to take her by the hand and lead her back into the security and affection of the room. Fiona seemed to be using improvisation to act out in a fairly concrete manner her verbally unexpressed fears.

So, in dozens of different ways like these, children spontaneously play out different aspects of their experience in ways which enable them to learn and gain reassurance.

DRAMA LEARNING AND TEACHING

In schools, teachers are employing similar ways of enabling the children to make discoveries: the Wendy house, the shop, the acted folk-tale and myth all assist.

As the children get older, games become a further extension of this play. One group of eleven-year-olds involved themselves in a situation in which they received a letter requesting them to board some transport destined eventually to take them to some remote planet where they found themselves isolated and having to begin to build a whole new community. Basically, it was a play situation and the children were absorbed in an imaginative adventure, but the teacher was a kind of catalyst assisting the class in the deepening of the experience and in their discoveries about relationships and social dilemmas. Sometimes, in setting up situations teachers have a real contribution to make towards helping the children extend their involvement, their imagination and their understanding. A group of fourteen-year-olds, after setting up a village community, found themselves playing roles in a public meeting called in order to protest against pollution of the local river from a nearby detergent factory. Depending on the role they found themselves playing, they had to appraise the problem and marshal the arguments for or against the various solutions suggested.

Sometimes such imaginative situations are set up with a minimum of preparation. At other times, they may involve elaborate data, equipment and rules. Everyone has come into contact with the game "Monopoly" and this is an example of improvisation in what has become known as "simulation". Our two basic elements, spontaneity and ingenuity in imaginative situations for the purpose of gaining insight, are very much in evidence.

In education generally there is a need for some practical means of exploring reality, a need to co-ordinate specialist skills and investigations, a point of focus where the individual and the group can find expression, and can experience the relationship between the various activities throughout the timetable. Some headmasters find it difficult to accept drama as anything other than an extra-curricular activity, or to associate it with anything beyond the annual school play.

At least one sometime Director of Education* looks upon the arts as best suited to the education of women, failing apparently to see the need for any opportunities where men and women can learn the building of relationships and come to an understanding of their differences in temperament.

A group of children were being observed by students. The children were in their last year of secondary school life and had had no previous drama experience. In the first few weeks of improvised drama work, the class seemed dull, lethargic and completely unresponsive. Some of the students, who were also working with the children on written English, declared to their tutor in the early stages, "If you're worried about their imagination, you needn't, because we've discovered they haven't got any." Only a few weeks

* See John Newsom's article in *The Observer*, 6 September 1964.

later, as a result of the improvisations in which the students worked with them, the same students declared, "These kids are better than we are."

In another instance, a retarded boy of fourteen at the end of a four-day holiday drama course, during which he had been difficult and apparently unresponsive, finally took part in an improvised play in front of parents and friends, and was so delighted at finding he could improvise effectively that he said in amazement, "Hey, I can talk."

Very often the children whom we regard as dull because they are unresponsive to the usual academic approach are in need of an imaginative awakening.

AN ACTOR TRAINING

So far, in most schools drama has not been seen as significant enough to be given a place, especially when staff are demanding more time for subjects which are respectable enough to be examined. For some educationalists, the examination takes the place of the opening night of the production in the theatre and similar excuses about lack of time for all except essentials are made. (By essentials they generally mean what the examination will ask, not what life will demand.) Yet, just as in the theatre improvisation helps the actor's overall confidence and final performance, so, in the learning process, ample experience has indicated that improvised drama, because it aids overall development of the personality, also improves the quality of examination work at all levels. With the highly intelligent, it helps to a surer development on a personal and emotional plane, leading to a more co-ordinated and balanced person.

In the teaching of drama, the process is also given another dimension. We not only wish to gain insight into social and political problems, but also into ourselves and how we react and feel. This kind of approach was pioneered by Stanislavsky. He was constantly at pains to help the actor draw upon what was spontaneous as well as imaginative and to help him to produce honest reactions rather than simply presenting a superficial and externalised act. He describes one such use of improvisation in *An Actor Prepares*:

"I shall stick the pin in a fold of this curtain and you are to find it."

In a moment he announced that he was ready.

Maria dashed on to the stage as if she had been chased. She ran to the edge of the footlights and then back again, holding her head with both hands, and writhing with terror. Then she came forward again, and then again went away, this time in the opposite direction. Rushing out toward the front she seized the folds of the curtain and shook them desperately, finally burying her head in them. This act she intended to represent looking for the brooch. Not finding it, she turned quickly and dashed off the stage, alternately holding her head or beating her breast, apparently to represent the general tragedy of the situation.

Those of us who were sitting in the orchestra could scarcely keep from laughing.

It was not long before Maria came running down to us in a most triumphant manner. Her eyes shone, her cheeks flamed.

"How do you feel?" asked the Director.

"Oh, just wonderful! I can't tell you how wonderful. I'm so happy," she cried, hopping around on her seat. "I feel just as if I had made my debut . . . really at home on the stage."

"That's fine," said he encouragingly, "but where is the brooch? Give it to me."

"Oh, yes," said she, "I forgot that."

"That is rather strange. You were looking hard for it, and you forgot it!"

We could scarcely look around before she was on the stage again, and was going through the folds of the curtain.

"Do not forget this one thing," said the Director warningly, "if the brooch is found you are saved. You may continue to come to these classes. But if the pin is not found you will have to leave the school."

Immediately her face became intense. She glued her eyes on the curtain, and went over every fold of the material from top to bottom, painstakingly, systematically. This time her search was at a much slower pace, but we were all sure that she was not wasting a second of her time and that she was sincerely excited although she made no effort to seem so.

"Oh, where is it? Oh, I've lost it."

This time the words were muttered in a low voice.

"It isn't there," she cried, with despair and consternation, when she had gone through every fold.

Her face was all worry and sadness. She stood motionless, as if her thoughts were far away. It was easy to feel how the loss of the pin had moved her.

We watched, and held our breath.

Finally the Director spoke.

"How do you feel now, after your second search?" he asked.

"How do I feel? I don't know." Her whole manner was languid, she shrugged her shoulders as she tried for some answer, and unconsciously her eyes were still on the floor of the stage. "I looked hard," she went on, after a moment.

"That's true. This time you really did look," said he. "But what did you do the first time?"

"Oh, the first time I was excited, I suffered."

"Which feeling was more agreeable, the first, when you rushed about and tore up the curtain, or the second, when you searched through it quietly?"

"Why, of course, the first time, when I was looking for the pin."

"No, do not try to make us believe that the first time you were looking for the pin," said he. "You did not even think of it. You merely sought to suffer, for the sake of suffering.

"But the second time you really did look. We all saw it; we understood, we believed, because your consternation and distraction actually existed.

"Your first search was bad. The second was good."

This verdict stunned her.

IMPROVISATION IN THE THEATRE

Joan Littlewood, with her Theatre Workshop company at Stratford East, developed her knowledge and understanding of Stanislavsky's ideas in her work on all her productions.

Members of the company reported in *Encore*, July 1960:

For the first week of rehearsals of *The Quare Fellow* we had no scripts. None of us had even read the play. We knew it was about prison life in Dublin, and that was enough for Joan. None of us had ever been in prison, and although we could all half-imagine what it was like, Joan set out to tell us more – the narrow world of steel, of stone, high windows and clanging doors, the love-hate between warder and prisoner, the gossip, the jealousy, and the tragedy – all the things that make up the fascination of dreariness. She took us up on to the roof of the Theatre Royal. All the grimy slate and stone made it easy to believe we were in a prison yard. We formed up in a circle, and imagined we were prisoners out on exercise. Round and round we trudged for what seemed like hours – breaking now and then for a quick smoke and furtive conversation. Although it was just a kind of game, the boredom and meanness of it all was brought home. Next, the "game" was extended – the whole dreary routine of washing out your cell, standing to attention, sucking up to the screws, trading tobacco, was improvised and developed. It began to seem less and less like a game, and more like real.

A few other companies use improvisation in some aspects of production, but within the theatre generally very few producers are using it to the full. Most would claim that they haven't time and that in a limited rehearsal period their main aim must be to get the play on. But the use of improvisation does not necessarily make rehearsals a longer process, and sometimes even the most practised and skilled directors could short-cut some of the difficulties arising in rehearsals if once they could be enabled to experience its value. Many actors are extremely suspicious and even afraid of improvisation because they feel it takes away the reassurance of the text in the hand or the memorized words and moves. It calls for a quick grasp of a situation and a fairly immediate response with the whole person, and where training has not developed this, more time is needed to build confidence. Thinking requires effort, concentration and practice, so it is true that the initial stages of improvisation are sometimes tentative, but the kind of assurance which follows the tentative stage is infinitely more valuable than the kind which rises from set patterns memorized.

ITS APPLICATION TO INDUSTRY

Some training courses for men and women from the business and industrial world are incorporating in their programmes situations involving role-playing as a means of finding solutions to, and understanding of, problems set. One such problem frequently given is to re-enact a situation in which one person undertakes the role of the employer faced with dismissing an employee whose role is played by another member of the group. Or in the case of a pay and productivity dispute, a situation is set up enabling the management to play the roles of the workers and the workers to take those of the management. In situations of this sort, it is possible to experience some of the feelings of both sides and some of the difficulties involved, so making follow-up discussion of much greater value.

Many more organizations could come to realize the full value and application that improvisation can have in affording opportunities for experience and insight on many levels.

IMPROVISATION AS THERAPY

As long ago as the beginning of the nineteenth century the Marquis de Sade was employing drama with his fellow inmates of the Charenton Lunatic Asylum, with what we would consider therapeutic effects. Today there is an increasing interest in improvised drama as a way of aiding all kinds of people in curing emotional, mental or other personality disturbances.

At The Henderson Hospital at Sutton in Surrey, as reported in *The Observer*, 31 January 1965, "treatment is designed through group and relationship therapy to fit very disturbed and delinquent individuals to work together on their minor psychological problems". One middle-aged woman, when asked what the hospital had done for her, said, "Well, I don't take the tablets any more – I have learned to put human relationships in their place." Isn't the group therapy found in drama improvisation the activity which will replace psychoanalysis? It draws upon the subconscious, it is introspective and has the advantage of being able to be shared and extroverted.

A few leaders in the probation service are recognizing that here is an approach which might enable both those on probation and officers to grasp and sort out difficulties more readily and effectively than they are able to in the straightforward interview. At one probation office, where improvisation was used with a small group of children, it was interesting to notice that some of these difficult youngsters who came most reluctantly under compulsion to the probation office for their interview arrived as much as an hour early for improvisation – a legitimate outlet for pent-up feelings.

These children started acting out a situation such as that in which they were all marooned on a desert island, and this developed freely as they spontaneously imagined they came across a castle or a tree or a boat. There was no set patter and situations developed largely from the spontaneous response of the subconscious. The children played whatever roles they felt like playing and brought in the woman probation officer, as and when they wanted, generally in the role of a police or mother figure. Apart from children having an opportunity of working out their own situations, these meetings also enabled the probation officer to build up her understanding of the children and their relationships. Couldn't the same benefits be derived at the adult level both with those on probation and those already committed to institutions like Borstals, remand homes and prisons?

People from a wide variety of backgrounds, both in education and theatre, are asking about improvisation, how to begin it, and the lines along which the work can be developed, and in this book we have tried to indicate something of its scope and direction. Constantly underlying the approach throughout the book is our belief in the link between drama and education.

We see acting as a central activity in the understanding of ourselves and our lives and, whether this is pursued professionally for the theatre or primarily as a means of education or re-education, we see the central activity of acting as improvisation.

CHAPTER 2

Acting and Responding

If acting is to have such emphasis in so many fields of activity, we must first of all face some of the fears and associations in peoples' minds.

For many people the term "acting" is used in a derogatory way – associated with the "illusory" rather than the "real". Isn't all acting phoney? How can there be any truth in it? What can it have to do with life? Isn't it all mere escapism, and aren't actors basically exhibitionists? Worse still – isn't it all positively dangerous to encourage situations in which the world of make-believe might overtake the world of reality?

First, we must try to decide what acting is. Acting is an interpretation, an impersonation of aspects of the human situation. It may involve playing the role of another person or it may require the imagined response of one's own person to a mood or set of circumstances. In either case, the qualities needed for the best acting are also those qualities required for the fullest living.

Both involve coming to terms with oneself, coming to terms with one's physical environment and learning how to manage relationships with other people. In all aspects of his being the actor needs to be sensitively tuned to be able to respond to whoever or whatever he encounters – and his responses must be within his control.

When an actor is playing, for instance, the role of Jimmy Porter in Osborne's *Look Back in Anger*, he needs to know which aspects of himself to use and how to use them. He needs to understand the physical conditions of single attic-room living and he needs to understand and be able to establish Jimmy's relationship with Alison, Helena, Cliff, Alison's parents and Hugh Tanner's mother.

This understanding takes place partly on a mental and imaginative level, but if his acting is to portray the situation with truth, he will have to understand with his whole being.

GOOD AND BAD ACTING

Truth in acting is not necessarily the representation of reality but rather the kind of acting which, by its spontaneity, enables us to see it as a true identification with life.

An exercise was given to a girl. She was asked to respond imaginatively in different ways to drinking from a number of cups. With the first she was asked to imagine she was drinking something pleasant. With the second she had to imagine she was uncertain, but found it was pleasant. With the third she was to take it that she knew it would be distasteful, and with the last she was to imagine that she was uncertain about it, but found it to be unpleasant.

A group of students was asked to watch and comment at the end on the "truth" of these reactions. Unknown to any of them, including the girl, the third cup, the "distasteful" one, contained vinegar, while the others held cold tea. So unpleasant was the vinegar that the girl spat it out and the comments of the onlookers were that this reaction was overplayed. It was her reaction to the fourth cup which was felt to be most real. The pattern seemed to be a question of responding, preparing a response, shock and control.

In other words, it is not necessarily the presentation of an actual bus conductor doing his usual job, nor is it the wife actually losing her temper with her husband, nor Hamlet's mother actually drinking poison: it is the actor who, by his insight and total understanding of the situation, re-creates the "life" at a given moment and in a given context, in a way in which our acceptance of it as "the real" is evoked. True acting may be larger than life, it may be smaller than life, it may be very well rehearsed or may be completely unrehearsed: the important thing always is for it to evoke our acceptance of it as valid at the time of its enactment. It may be seen in comedy, tragedy, farce, revue or any other medium – each of these will call for its own particular approach to acting, conditioned by the kind of interpretation demanded by each form and each age.

An actor's training, therefore, cannot be confined to the isolated techniques of voice and body, but must give considerable emphasis to the discovery of ways of creating those qualities which can be identified with life and of evoking a true response. His training would also need to include a development of his ability to interpret the life around him and of associating it with the life of a given text. All this he will need to learn to co-ordinate within himself and with the theatre group.

KNOWING OR BEING TOLD?

For the actor's understanding of a situation with his whole being, it is not sufficient for him simply to be "told" by someone else:

when we are told something we understand it with the mind only – total knowing is a matter of personal experience involved in living through a situation. A young actress was told by her producer a point of interpretation. He continued to reiterate the point at almost every rehearsal, until she suddenly exclaimed, "Now I understand it!" The producer complained, "But I've been telling you this for weeks." She looked at him simply and said, "I know, but I've had to find out for myself!" It is this finding out for oneself which enables the actor to comprehend the situation at all levels.

Some actors do play certain roles without consciously making themselves aware of the situation wholly – in fact, they give a convincing interpretation of the part because the role calls for, or they choose to give the part, only those qualities which are already uppermost in their personalities (consciously or subconsciously). If the actor restricts himself to playing roles with this limited outlook, then he is denying his development both as an actor and as a person.

ACTING REQUIRES COMMUNICATION

While there is undoubtedly a need for the actor to communicate with his fellow actors and with the audience, this is more in the nature of a sharing of his role-playing rather than a showing or showing-off. Mere exhibitionism is a self-centred form of acting and in its assertion of the self denies discovery, which can only follow from a more generous approach.

Similarly, the more introverted form of acting, in which the actor looks at himself and uses his acting as a means of self-admiration, denies his growth. In this narcissistic outlook the individual is much too concerned with the pleasure of his present state to be able to derive any benefit from acting with others. The kind of looking at oneself which is necessary for the actor is that which comes from heightened awareness. It seeks to understand the workings of the human personality in order that a fuller experience at a personal and group level may evolve.

Another kind of limitation is seen in the actor who plays his roles on the stage with efficiency and insight and yet outside the play remains a strictly limited person. He seems to take none of his insight from art into life.

All these people are specialists in the narrowest sense. The function of any art, and especially drama, is to contribute to the fuller development of the individual. At its best, drama calls upon actors to respond to living in order to interpret the play fully, and conversely this response to the re-creation in the acted play enables all participants to respond more fully to life.

THREE KINDS OF ESCAPISM

This does not deny that acting enjoyed in the doing, or experienced as an audience, is not a means of escape. What it does, however, is attempt to define the kind of escape. Kenneth Tynan, in one of his *Observer* articles,* raised the question whether it was not as legitimate to escape through drugs as through a large bank balance or church group: "A connection is established between dope and religion, and a question is implicitly posed: if the aim of life is happiness why is it more respectable to achieve it by pumping salvation into the soul, or income into the bank, than by pumping heroin into the blood stream?" We surely need to see that there are different kinds of escapism and that, in order to assess them, we have to judge them by their results. The kind of escape which we get from drugs means very often that, although our experience may be heightened for a time, we return to the non-drugged state finding it less tolerable than before, so that the escape has been no escape and we only crave for more and more of the drug.

A more common experience is that of "forgetting oneself" for a short period, through either a film or a book, or a drink, the return from which finds us unchanged, and in a situation which is almost identical with that we experienced before "escaping".

The most valuable form of escape for the human being is surely that which may well help us to forget for a while the situation around us, but that by its very nature gives some insight or develops awareness, so that when we return we bring something constructive which enables us to live on in the human situation with a greater sense of understanding and appreciation. This is not a substitute for everyday living, nor is it a means of pleasantly dreaming of a world free from problems in which someone like us will play the leading part. In any situation pursued for any length of time we find ourselves so close to the details that we become in danger of losing sight of the whole or getting it out of perspective. What we

* 26 February 1961.

need is a means of stepping back from our situation and of viewing it from as many different angles and distances as possible, in order to return with a fuller realization of its significance.

The dramatic experience is an intensification of living experience, realized by the selection and reordering of significant moments, and it exists in the communication between actors and audience physically present in one place. This communication takes place at every level: mental, emotional, physical, visual, aural and aesthetic.

During rehearsals the actor practises tuning himself to the part he is playing, and the part he is playing in relation to the other actors in the roles they are representing. With time and experience, he is able also to tune to the other actors and the audience at one and the same time.

There is an apparent paradox here, which is worth attention. During the portrayal of the role the actor has aimed to identify himself with the part he is playing, but practice has led him to be able to develop his awareness to the point at which this can be achieved while he is still retaining control. His awareness is such that he may, paradoxically, forget his audience while knowing he is communicating with them. The complex nature of man's sphere of awareness is seen wherever the situation calls for response on different levels of attention at the same time. A driver of a car may be engrossed in a conversation, but part of his awareness – it may only be the fringe – is sensitive to the road, the movement of other transport and the operation of the controls of the vehicle.

USING AND LOSING ONESELF

Many people concerned with acting seem at some stage to face this problem of identification and how fully they should become immersed in any part. They seem worried by the thought that if they become too involved in the part they will lose themselves and possibly their control of the situation. This idea may be encouraged by certain emotional films in which an actor, playing a part, becomes obsessed by the role especially when it contains some elements of violence. What is being exploited here is a pathological state, and this should not be confused with an investigation into representational acting. Often such is the emotional impact of these films that the deranged mental state is made to appear as if brought on by the acting, whereas in fact this acting is another aspect of role-playing noticed in some kinds of mental unbalance. For example, many people have played Othello, identifying themselves with the character, but their awareness of this as an acted situation prevents them from actually smothering Desdemona. Only the psychopath actually wishes to carry this out.

This anxiety about loss of control is sometimes complicated by an awareness, but inadequate understanding, of theories associated with two outstanding influences in modern theatre: Stanislavsky and Brecht. In fact, where these two differ is in their approach to character creation. Stanislavsky's work led to an emphasis of the subjective, personal approach; Brecht's work has led to the emphasis being placed on an objective, more impersonal, way of building the character. But both are in agreement in their demand for concentration, and when we understand the nature of man's imagination and his ability to focus attention we do not need to pursue a false antithesis. What we need to do is to spend time in practising to develop concentration in acting, and bring greater insight and intelligence to our understanding of the requirements of the play. We should not be asking, "How involved must I become in this part?" but "What kind of concentrated approach to characterization will best suit this text?" The actor achieves this experience partly on his own and partly with his company.

It is possible, however, for an actor playing a part in the theatre to continue playing this role at other times. Peter O'Toole studies most of his parts with such intensity that he carries away aspects of his current theatre role with him into situations away from the stage. It is clear, nevertheless, that at no time is he in confusion as to when he is acting the part in the context of the play and, similarly, when he carries the character with him at other times he retains his understanding of the off-stage situation.

For instance, while he was playing Bamforth in *The Long and the Short and the Tall* he took part in a discussion on the play organized by *Encore*. In this discussion his vocabulary, phraseology and manner were strongly reminiscent of Bamforth, yet he remained aware of the time and the need to be ready for the evening's performance. One part of him was clearly aware of the discussion while another part of his concentration retained the character. This illustrates the fact that it is possible to be immersed in a part to the extent of carrying it beyond the theatre situation, yet retaining control and awareness. Both control and concentration are essential in the building of any characterization, and if an actor loses his control or his concentration his performance will not be truthful.

The kind of performance which passed as acting in earlier generations is happily less admired today – though still seen in some productions. That is the solo or star approach, where the "leading man" gave the audience the full performance and no one else mattered. Kean wrote to the stage-manager of the Croydon Theatre before the opening of *The Merchant of Venice* and *The Iron Chest*, "Sir, I shall not require any rehearsals for my plays, but be particular in your selection of Wilford, he is all important to me." This all importance is indicated in Wilford's account of the interview at the theatre. When Kean sent for him, Stirling, who played the role, asked, "What do you wish me to do?"

"While in the library scene, sink gradually on your right knee with your back to the audience. When I place my hand on your head mind you keep your eyes fixed on mine."

"Is that all, sir?"

"Yes – do whatever you like after that; it will be all the same to me."*

Such an experience seems almost incredible today. What we are having to realize more and more is that acting, like living, is a combination of the individual and the group approach. Individual talents are co-ordinated and developed within the community. Drama is the only art form which fully recognizes man's gregarious nature. While emphasizing the living-group activity, it enables him to communicate and respond as a total being.

* Quoted by Norman Marshall in *The Producer and the Play* (Macdonald).

CHAPTER 3

Living and Responding

Acting is an experiment in living, to look at it from another point of view. Learning how to live comes through experiencing. Improvisation is a means of exploring in which we create conditions where imaginative group and personal experience is possible. It is the spontaneous human response to an idea or ideas, or a set of conditions.

MAN AS A UNIFIED BEING

In most of our approaches to life, whether through science or through education in schools, and even through the training of the actor, we tend to look at man as a subject for analysis. In science, man becomes a study for one aspect: medical science, social science, or psychology, and education concerns itself with parts: physical education, religious education, arts education or training on the abstract mental level. Even the actor finds his tuition periods subdivided often exclusively into voice production, movement, dance, singing and so forth. So all through life there is very little attempt to look at man as a whole being, and inadequate concern to bring together these elements of training in development of the total personality. While some emphasis will always need to be placed upon differing aspects of development, we need to ensure that we spend adequate time in the unified living situation. From time to time we need to re-examine whatever aspects of existence we are working on and be sure that we have recognized their relationship to man in his environment. Kenneth Walker quotes the Indian tale:

> The elephant was in a dark house: some Hindus had brought it for exhibition.
>
> In order to see it, many people were going, every one, into that darkness.
>
> As seeing it with the eye was impossible, each one was feeling it in the dark with the palm of his hand.
>
> The hand of one fell on its trunk: he said, "This creature is like a water-pipe."

The hand of another touched its ear: to him it appeared to be like a fan.

Since another handled its leg, he said, "I found the elephant shape to be like a pillar."

Another laid his hand on the back: he said, "Truly this elephant was like a throne."

Similarly, when anyone heard a description of the elephant, he understood it only in respect of the part that he had touched.

On account of the diverse place of view their statements differed: one man entitled it "dal" another "alif".

If there had been a candle in each one's hand, the difference would have gone out of their words.*

If we really believe that the "proper study of mankind is man", the best way of studying him is as he responds in relationships with people and things. There must be ample time devoted to allowing opportunity for the candles to be lit to enable us to see man as a whole.

MAN AS A UNIQUE BEING

While we are classifying man in the analytical process, stressing the common factors and trends in human behaviour, we must not lose sight of the unique quality of every individual. The body of human knowledge which enables us to classify and clarify various facets of human nature needs to have something to offset it, so that we recognize that in every man and woman there is a singular combination of the varying facets. This means that every single human being is a subject for research, and somehow we must accept opportunities in the growing process for everyone to be able to find out about himself and to discover the particular peculiarities of himself in relation to other people.

This may seem disturbing, for this concept of the unique nature of the individual means abandoning the idea of a safety measure of "normality". Society is nearly always unwilling to recognize anything or anyone that seems different, but this is an attitude which only adds to the conflict and complexity of man's existence, making individuals afraid of being different, and individuals afraid of the different. What we need to inculcate more is a sense of wonder at

* Kenneth Walker: *The Diagnosis of Man* (Penguin).

the uniqueness of the individual. We must learn to put this in place of the fear which results in the sneer leading to opposition and aggression.

Not only is every person different – every person has also unparalleled possibilities and potential. Everyone begins life with his particular heredity and personality make-up, modified by unique factors of environment which in turn bring their own variety of pressures, opportunities or lack of opportunities in the great range of experience that each individual undergoes. These factors are given further variety by individual differences in the rate of development which in turn contribute to the variety of human personality.

Generalized statements there may well be about the human situation, but we must always be on our guard lest we attempt to make human beings fit them, instead of using them to gain understanding of the individual. We all gain considerable comfort from realizing that we are not totally in a world unknown and unshared by others. We can gain help by talking about, and discovering, our similarities, but we should also feel that we can discuss and share our differences. There is a kind of paradox in which we need to appreciate the uniqueness of ourselves and of every other human being and that, though unique, we have had and are having experiences similar to others.

Poetry and the novel offer an opportunity for some understanding of the need to break down the fear that "I am alone in my difference: everyone else is together in their similarity". Both the private and the group level of experience are important, and in making discoveries about both these spheres of our life we have to accept the fact that only the individual can adequately discover himself for himself. This is a different kind of understanding from the accepted scientific knowledge where, once we have found how to split the atom, we can go on from generation to generation, if we wish, splitting it in the same way. On the human level, every single person in every generation has to have the opportunity of being able to find out about himself for himself.

The objective study of man in the social situation tends to leave part of man out of consideration. It has either to be a discussion of the situation after the event (for instance, the juvenile court or probation office), when rationalization is likely to take place, or an impartial observer viewing a situation from the touch-line (such as the social worker), from where it is only possible to grasp the externalized manifestations.

Drama is the only form in which we can fully use man in the exploration of himself in the living situation. Whether the living experience is recorded in a text or is set in motion by one or more ideas, its fullest discovery as personal experience must be realized through improvisation. Through drama, those experiencing the intensified situation can gain insight within controlled conditions.

Science has tended in the past to distrust the subjective approach at all levels, believing it to be too prone to prejudice and self-deception. In improvisation, indulgence in a world of fantasy or self-deception is still possible and may well take place at some stages, but as it is taking place in a group situation, the final understanding arrived at will be part of exploration with others. This allows for the individual to work through the stage of fantasy or self-deception, and to reach his state of insight in concert with others. When the individual accepts the fact that the result of his personal research into his own working is to enable him to improve his own working, he quickly realizes the importance of identifying misrepresentations. So, improvisation exists not just in the imagination, but is lived and moved physically alongside other human beings, in time and space. The feet of those improvising are constantly on the ground, sustained by other actors who help to ensure that all claims, hopes, fears and so on are referred to some clarified human response.

Throughout improvisation response will be from and with every part of the person, even though constantly attention will be focused on a particular aim.

Aims and values of Improvisation

GROWTH OF THE INDIVIDUAL AS A PERSON

In the early stages of dramatic improvisation it is usual to encounter self-consciousness and embarrassment. This is largely because we are overcome with shyness at being asked to respond in an imaginative world! So the first aim is to release the tension, and the best way of doing this is to develop powers of concentration. What we shall be trying to do is to enable the members of the groups to become absorbed in the activity they are pursuing instead of, as

may well happen at first, being concerned with themselves undertaking the activity. Gradually, too, we would hope to lose this self-
consciousness altogether and substitute an awareness of oneself,
which can aid personal development where self-consciousness
hindered it.

Linked closely with absorption is a sharpening of the powers of
observation. This means not only looking with a keener eye but
listening with a keener ear and responding with keener senses all
round, including feeling with greater sensitivity. We should aim at
a greater awareness of size and shape, texture and quality, and
senses sharpened to detail. Then we can begin to see one thing in
terms of another and to notice the relationship between one thing
and another, growing into a fuller grasp of the value and meaning
in symbolism and imagery.

This process begun, it is easier to reinstate the work of the
imagination. Every one of us has a keen imagination in early childhood, but the structure of our society and relationships tends to
make us feel less happy about it. Gradually we become anxious to
suppress it or hide it until finally the power is lost altogether. Our
day-to-day existence conspires against the practice of imagination.
We quickly associate it with the fanciful and somehow the concrete
world of reality is made to seem more worthy. We are fed daily by
television programmes of all kinds which do the imagining for us
and, consequently, what imagination does remain is relegated to
the hidden world of day-dreams and nightmares. Yet imagination
is a quality more than ever required in this era of increasing activity
and advancement. Every kind of development must have some
imagination. In the home it is desirable for decoration, the buying
of furniture, preparation of food; we need it in the purchase of our
clothes and even in the organization of our holidays and leisure
time. Every development in industry requires some degree of
imagination. It is required more and more in building and architecture, technical improvements and throughout community life.
Imagination can enrich the existence of all on an industrial, technical, social, and personal plane, and acting aids imaginative
growth.

Improvisation is a means of training people to think. It aims at
the inculcation of clear mental habits and the training of the expression of these thoughts in a concise and orderly way. Because it
places people in a human situation involving other people, it calls

for fairly quick thinking and at times for different levels of thought at one and the same time. Decisions have to be made by the individual in the situation, but because it is an experimental situation, he can learn by his errors or adjust to the utilization of his mistakes. In a world of ubiquitous advertising clarity of thought is in danger of being blunted, and practice of thought response at different levels is essential.

It is, however, important to distinguish this kind of thinking from intellectualizing, divorced from the human situation. What is required during improvisation is thinking within a situation, or thinking about a situation after it has been experienced. In so many other fields we are expected to think intellectually about something we have never experienced, whereas here the experience comes first, or accompanies the thought. It is sometimes possible to reach a greater degree of truth from acting out a situation, even acting it out a second time, than is possible when called upon to explain it in detached conversation.

Thinking can lead to expression of these thoughts, but it can also show the wisdom of silence. As understanding develops we should become more aware of the contribution and interest of others, and so learn the value of listening and of giving ourselves through listening. In improvisation another dimension in acting becomes clear. Acting is not only moving or talking and reacting mechanically at a given cue, but becomes more of a living response arrived at from a continuous thought pattern.

Most of the aims so far mentioned seem desirable in any form of artistic or general training, but improvisation aims to combine these with a development and training of the emotions. If anyone is to live and respond fully, he needs to know both how and why his feelings work as they do. It is true that we know more about how to get to the moon than how individual emotions work, and we come to be afraid of areas of uncertain knowledge. Yet surely the only way we are going to come to any grasp of emotions in the living situation is to be aware of them under experimental and imaginative conditions. We are all expected to love and be loved, but there is never any opportunity of preparing ourselves to find out about love until we are in the actual situation. And we need to go farther, for it is not only important to know how to love but we must know also what it is to hate. We need to find out what happens when we get angry, what it is like to be sensitive and to show sensitivity. These can be explored in a controlled situation which will help us to understand how this neglected aspect of our being works in relation to the whole person. It is no good our leaving this part of our development to chance, simply because it is difficult or little known, and then looking surprised or superior when later we find things have not worked out for the most balanced frame of living. Improvisation is attempting to provide a training in getting on with other people and some understanding of what happens in a breakdown of relationships.

This is partially linked with our understanding of the build-up of tension and the best use of human energy. We learn to relax fully (that is with body, mind and emotion) and discover how to keep relaxed with as much of the personality as possible, ensuring that the effort is properly directed and adequately organized.

All this develops our understanding, helping us not only to experience but to see this experience in relation to other things and other people. Fears and insecurities are the result of, or conditioned by, lack of understanding, so that the more we can discover why this human situation takes place or how we can deal with another situation, the more we can live confidently. Understanding of this kind involves not only the mind but the whole personality, seeking to bring greater insight into the whole of the human situation. Furthermore, when we have the grasp of a situation with our whole being, it means that conscious effort at memory work is unnecessary. What is learned in the fullest way is unlikely to be forgotten. Emphasis is placed upon the deepest knowing and away from mere repetition for the sake of rote learning.

Understanding is taking place on a dual plane, for at the same time as we are finding out about ourselves and our personal relationships with other people we are also learning to understand others so that we can realize more fully in what ways they are like us and in what ways they are different. Improvisation is a group activity and learning within the group situation leads to a realization both of man's independence and his interdependence. The sense of community thus has an opportunity for growth. The group in improvisation works in a different way from the team in a game. In most games we are concerned with specific physical skills and agilities, and the aim is to play upon the shortcomings of our opponent and to sift out any weaknesses in our own team. The co-operation which we get in team games is on a very limited level and usually attention is drawn away from the human aspect. The contrast in improvised drama is seen in the fact that the stronger work with the weaker in a living situation, helping them through their weakness and building confidence in a non-competitive situation. When one group shares its work with another there is a further development of understanding and groups quickly realize that the emphasis lies away from display.

It is clear, then, that opportunity throughout improvisation is in those who participate taking part on two important levels – doing and being. Groups learn how to employ feelings which elsewhere might remain frustrated in expression. There is an emphasis upon the active participation of everyone and this participation is through "being". There are many useful means of gaining experience in a passive and substitute way, but drama calls for the living response and resourcefulness. We are, in fact, employing a means as old as man himself. Quite naturally, adult primitive man attempts to cope with the elements and the human predicament through taking on an impersonation in dance or drama, or both, of the thunder or the sun, and attempts to come to some understanding of, or with, those powers which seem to him to be beyond his plane of existence. In more sophisticated society the approach of impersonation seems a built-in response in helping to enable every one of us to keep the world in manageable proportions. The young child literally steps into mother's shoes, puts on her clothing and carries out her duties, in order to grasp what that situation is really like. Another approach taken by the small child is to substitute someone or something else for himself. Children put their dolls and playthings through all the indignities to which they are subjected, and it is an enormous help for them in their mastering of the difficult learning process. But it is not only children who cope with the unpleasant this way. Most people find they can cope with a difficult situation better by acting it out later, bringing out the comedy, which, while they were actually experiencing the initial situation, never occurred to them. Or we mimic the people who have got the better of us and it all helps us in gaining a better perspective.

More specifically, improvised drama helps us to understand the movement of the body in relation to everything else. Part of all self-consciousness is physical, and through improvisation greater free-dom and co-ordination of bodily movement is obtained, because we are conscious of putting the body into imaginative situations and developing freedom in control.

Similarly, because much of the work involves us in talking, we gain confidence in a flow of intelligent speech. The use of language is extended, together with dexterity in the manner of expression. It is possible to learn the special subtleties and variations of meaning which the spoken word has over the written. This aids clearer communication and avoidance of misunderstandings. Most of the stress in the majority of our educational programmes has so far been placed upon the written word. Through improvisation there is a real opportunity to come to an awareness of the difference between written and spoken communication. The use of language varies in different situations, and in the variety of the subjects of improvisation there is a chance to realize how vocabulary, word order, and images vary from circumstance to circumstance.

Because the response takes place as the situation proceeds, spontaneity is more assured. This means that, on every level, there can be a freshness and honesty which is often unusual. The conventional learned response very readily leads to a rather jaded reaction, but here there is usually pleasure in the unknown.

Much of the work brings an involvement with an occupation or a concern with a person, leading to a looking beyond oneself, so that there are great moments of surprise at what one has achieved. Individuals discover their own potential. They find they are capable of things which neither they nor others realized.

None of these values is achieved in isolation, but each one will build together, giving a true sense of security to the individual. This is a certainty which arises from a real sense of knowing, rather than remembered and unapplied facts. In a friendly atmosphere there has been a gradual ridding of tensions which become replaced by a genuine and lasting self-confidence.

In the early stages, when an individual is particularly insecure, improvisation may well add to his fears. He sometimes feels that he is being "got at", because he is given a situation to follow through in which he will reveal, most likely, part or all of himself. This fear is linked with his self-consciousness and can be overcome both by his growing concentration and absorption in what is being done, and the solidarity which rises from being a member of a group. Gradually, as the individual realizes that everyone, especially the leader, is present in a sympathetic manner, he becomes more released. The leader can help build self-confidence by himself taking part in the improvisations. At other times he can build his own understanding of individuals within the group by his sensitive observation of the work. He can then be kept in touch with the needs and the development of his groups. People soon realize that, while they are revealing themselves, this act in itself is part of the growth and part of the way of ensuring growth.

GROWTH OF THE INDIVIDUAL AS AN ACTOR

Every element of personal development will aid the actor in his art. Conversely, because of the nature of acting and the dramatic experience, each extension of skill and perception in this field can aid the individual in living.

With the greater development within the individual of his observation and understanding of people, we should improve capacity for the interpretation of a character, and this, together with additional skill in movement and words, can lead to greater dexterity in the building of characterization. Improved concentration and a more lively imagination help him to be able to sustain a role more easily and effectively and give the capacity for retention of the imaginative truth of a situation. The actor has to learn to draw from himself in relation to an idea or a dramatic text, and know himself as a creative artist working as a member of a team.

By understanding the nature of dramatic writing, as distinct from other kinds of writing, he should begin to see a text as that which calls for living expression. He enjoys developing his capacity for getting inside dramatic writing, which leads him to a rediscovery of drama of the present day and of the past. Experience in one text should lead him out and on to experience in others.

All this work both with and without texts should help the person who is acting to come to an awareness of shape, not just with the intellect, but with the whole person. He begins to see that form and shape can be experienced and expressed in a variety of ways; physically and mentally he responds to rhythm as expressed in sound, in movement and in other aspects of life. From the group sensitivity and the knowledge of subtlety and variety of meaning should spring a keener sense of timing and pattern.

Above all, there is the satisfaction of working as a member of a creative team which helps him leave behind any notions of mere self-display. There is a greater sense of achievement in recognizing and developing the actor's own potential as an individual creating with others.

So much for the theoretical background to improvisation. In the next two sections the approach is more practical.

PART II

IMPROVISING
without using a text

CHAPTER 4

Beginning and Developing Improvisation

There is no set formula or rule-of-thumb technique for approaching improvisation. It has a myriad of different approaches, applications and points of emphasis, and because it can be used with people of all ages and people of differing backgrounds, it is vital for whoever is leading to regard the first improvisation sessions as an opportunity to "tune in" to the group. From this he can gain some idea of the needs, the rate of development and the kind of material which is most likely to prove profitable.

WHAT EQUIPMENT IS NEEDED?

Given a group, all that is essential is space. The size of the space depends on the size of the group and how active they are likely to be. Adequate room for movement is important, but it does not want to be too large, to lose the easy atmosphere necessary throughout all this work. Put to it, of course, almost any space can be used. Large groups can be cramped into small, restricted areas, small groups can be lost in vast halls, but where conditions are not advantageous it is vital for the leader to recognize this at the outset and plan his programme with some attempt at minimizing the awkward effects of the area. Should there be a formal platform or stage as part of the space, it is as well to regard it simply as an additional area for movement and avoid any suggestion of it being the "showing place". Levels, props, costume, lighting, can all be introduced as and when they seem desirable.

WHERE DO WE BEGIN?

When thinking about the early improvisation sessions we have to bear in mind the need to overcome self-consciousness in the groups, so that there is a need to go for ideas which will readily lead to absorption. As a rule, it helps to take something which is as near the everyday experience of the group as possible, in order that they can find themselves on familiar ground at the outset. Of course, with children at certain ages, or with any age group at certain stages of development, it might be best to work in the world of pure imagination or fantasy. Some groups will respond best to material which suggests considerable activity or excitement, while others will feel happier given something which appears less demanding. Much depends on the kind of group as to whether we begin obviously inside their everyday experience or whether self-consciousness is better overcome by taking them outside themselves and their circumstances.

When a group is made up of individuals who do not know one another, we need some work designed to introduce them. This, tackled early, can often prevent barriers being built up and ensure an easy, amicable atmosphere for later work. Where there is already a difficult relationship or lack of relationship evident, this early work might be best carried out on an individual level, that is to say, everyone working simultaneously but solo.

We need to go to the first meeting prepared to be flexible in approach. Have lots of ideas, probably short in themselves, which can be used to find the best way in. The material will need to have ample variety. If the group are obviously physically self-conscious when they first meet each other, a beginning might be made with everyone sitting down. When people seem vocally self-conscious, they might respond better to silent improvisations from which words, phrases and sentences can gradually be built. With larger groups crowds can easily become unmanageable or unwieldy, and perhaps it is as well to leave this sort of work until later on.

WHAT IS THE POINT OF PLANNING?

The aim should be to view the work over a definite period. The length of the period will depend upon conditions, but should be long enough to enable some clear development to take place. There is a need for a clear conception of aims, both long term and immediate, but, of course, we have to be prepared to modify the plan in the light of session-by-session experience. Even before meeting the group, it is good to have alternative plans so that if things do not work out as at first imagined there is another scheme ready to be put into operation. This will help to prevent the leader being put off his stride by the unexpected situation. Within the overall plan each session must have its well-thought-out place, and within each session each improvisation and phase will build to the immediate aim. So there will be some sense of shape at all times and this will enable each session to give the participants a sense of satisfaction. Older or more confident groups will need to experience development of the work right from the start. On the other hand, those with a different background and different needs may well derive satisfaction from exploration in a way which seems to show little progression. It is important that whoever is leading remains sensitive to the needs of his group, so that he can allow adequate time for what might seem chaotic adventures. Without hurrying these opening stages, he has to realize when the moment for elementary shaping arrives. Alternatively, it is just as important that a group should not be kept at this stage of chaotic adventuring when they could be working and achieving more through purposeful planning.

WHERE DOES THE MATERIAL COME FROM?

When a great French mime was asked by one of his students, looking for subject-matter, "What shall I take?" he is reputed to have told him, "You have all the world to choose from." Because drama is dealing with living, there is, in fact, no aspect of man's experience which does not have the possibility of exploration in improvisation. The main task of the leader is to look around and decide upon a theme or set of themes. Each session, depending on its length, can take one or more threads of experience which can be explored in a variety of ways: through movement, sound, speech, or a combination of any or all of these. These may be worked on as an end in themselves or as a preparation for building up a more complex scene or scenes. Towards the end of the session this sense of achievement we have been talking about can be aided by the drawing together of these strands in some unified improvisation.

HOW LARGE SHOULD THE GROUP BE?

There is no ideal size for a group, but fifteen to twenty people has been found a convenient number, giving opportunity for adequate individual knowledge and sufficient experience with larger numbers. For working purposes, the large group will be divided into smaller groups depending upon the aim and nature of the work. The group can work as individuals, in pairs, in threes, in small groups of five or six, or larger groups. In practice, it has been found that group work in threes is particularly convenient, since in threes the responsibility is not resting so obviously on one person and yet there is encouragement derived from being in the group. Work in pairs has definite advantages for some kinds of work, but is a disadvantage at other times, while work in fours tends to divide itself into two pairs.

HOW MUCH CAN BE ACHIEVED IN ONE SESSION?

Just as there is an infinite variety of materials and an infinite variety of methods of approach, so the arrangement of each session can have an ample variety. There are, however, certain elements which each session needs to embody. Unless this work flows naturally out of other activity of a similar kind, it will be important to recognize that some preparation or introduction is necessary if people are to respond easily and get the most out of what is being done. The first part should be designed to help free the body, the mind and the imagination, so that activities would include the loosening up of each of these aspects of the person. The material here can be associated with the theme chosen. Sometimes, the use of percussion or recorded music may be found to stimulate the work.

The introductory work should lead naturally into the improvisations planned for the rest of the session. The main section of any particular session will be built round the specific aim and can involve a variety of approaches to the aspect of the work being emphasized. Here activities will tend to be carried out in smallish groups, these groups sometimes working at their individual pace and sometimes progressing on a more definitely controlled line. The theme or themes selected will help in shaping throughout.

It is helpful to all concerned if the last part of each improvisation period can gather together the main aspects which have been explored. Usually, this will mean building a scene, either in small groups or the various groups coming together in one main improvisation. Adequate time would have to be allowed not only for the preparation and development of this scene or scenes but also for the final playing through, giving expression to a culmination and assessment of the overall experience.

Time spent on each part of the work will vary from week to week. Sometimes preliminary work may involve more emphasis than the others. In later sessions there may be occasions when the whole time would be used in preparing a united effort. Leaders will try to ensure that each meeting of the group develops its own rhythm of strenuous activity and quieter periods and a good leader will aim to ensure that there is an overall balance. Most sessions will contain some periods of total relaxation. These should be led into as naturally as possible and can often come into the imaginative pattern. Relaxation best follows periods of vigorous activity or strenuous effort, imaginative or physical, and will involve the whole group lying or sitting and feeling the tension released from every muscle group throughout the body. There will be some effort, too, to ensure a mental calm as well, so that there can be co-ordination between all aspects of the person.

WHAT IS THE ROLE OF THE LEADER?

The "leader" is the person organizing the session. He may be a producer, teacher, youth leader, actor, psychologist, probation officer or any other person interested. His function is not an authoritarian one, for he is more of an agent who sets up conditions in which discovery can be made. It is he who has planned the overall programme and thought through each session in detail. He aims at keeping an atmosphere in which personal and group discoveries can most easily be made. While steering the course, he tries to maintain an awareness of any worthwhile diversions, side-roads, and explorations which would call for a modification of time or direction schedule. There may be occasions when he will want to aid confidence by taking part with the group in movement or vocal improvisations, and there will be other times when he will realize that the personal discoveries of the people in the group demand that he make himself particularly inconspicuous.

He should regard himself as one of the group rather than seeing himself and the group as separate entities. In some cases where the leader is already known to everyone this may mean building a new relationship. It will, however, help the group to come to accept him as a fellow explorer, and even the conditions he sometimes sets and the questions he raises will be presented in a manner suggesting that he is interested in what people have derived from the experience or in what they feel about the work of others. He will have his own views and comments to make, but offered in the same spirit as a contribution from any other member of the group. When his wisdom or experience is greater than the other members', this will be readily apparent without the need for the adoption of any kind of exclusive role for the sake of authority.

HOW DO WE BEGIN?

When first meeting the group, it helps confidence if the person arranging the session knows he has too much material, and that his task will be to select from his carefully prepared work as he sees how the response is developing. Improvisations are worked out purely to help to build confidence and to promote an easy atmosphere. The development points may well be few, and even with fairly advanced and responsive groups it is wise at this stage not to look at any of the work of individual or groups in isolation. It is a useful aim to give everyone taking part some experience in the medium and the manner of working, so that by the end of the time everyone can have found his own level of response.

Some groups will become absorbed very quickly, while others will need more patience, and their lack of concentration may manifest itself in self-conscious giggles and laughter. When this occurs it is most helpful to everybody if the leader can accept the situation calmly and even provide opportunities for further release. Supposing a serious situation has been suggested, and some groups are seen fooling about or not taking it seriously, the leader might suggest that the improvisation is repeated, with everybody "sending it up", or making it a comic situation. Usually, this will help everybody to work their self-consciousness out. On the other hand, self-consciousness may show itself in shyness or hanging back, or more definite playing-up, and again the leader with the flexible programme can make adjustments, giving adequate time for everyone to "tune in". We are dealing with human development and there is bound to be the need to exercise patience. Where there are isolated "pockets of resistance", without drawing attention to them the leader might divide up these individuals, placing each one with a more absorbed group. Usually two or more absorbed people will draw in another person less sure of himself and give him the confidence he really needs.

In the first session the person leading may be surprised at the lack of success of some material which he has selected, because he was sure of its interest to the people he is working with. The case may be that it is not the material which is at fault, but that he has, in fact, to allow more time for the group to tune in to the kind of experiences they are being asked to undertake. Usually one is better advised to ask the group to work on small amounts of improvisation at any time, and he must expect to use a good number of short scenes in his first meetings. Some groups will organize the change of scene for themselves, starting on one set of ideas and characters and flowing naturally into a completely different situation. The place, the time, the characters, may switch without warning, and this kind of response would help the leader to discover a great deal about his group and will guide him in preparing future programmes. Whatever the case, clarity of instruction and simplicity of detail are always important.

Some possible Preliminary Sessions

Here are five possible ways of beginning with different kinds of groups:

I. WITH A MIXED GROUP OF ELEVEN-YEAR-OLDS

At the outset the group could be gathered round to explain that they were going to hear a story which they would afterwards act. The story might go something like this:

"One of the sons of the great Greek god Zeus was Perseus. Perseus wanted to show what a good warrior he was and so promised to bring back the head of one of the three monsters known as Gorgons, which had serpents for hair, and had the power of killing anybody who looked at them. Only one of them was mortal and her name was Medusa.

"To help him on his adventure, Perseus had winged sandals which made him able to fly, a special helmet which turned him invisible, and a bronze shield which shone so brightly that it gave a clear reflection. When he came to the Gorgons he used his shield as a mirror, so that he would not be killed by looking at the Gorgon, and with one sharp blow of his sword he cut off Medusa's head, put it into his special wallet and flew back to his home, pursued by the other two Gorgons, who were not fast enough to catch him up."

Once the leader has told the story he can explain that first time through everyone will take the part of Perseus and in the first part of the session everyone can practise putting on the special sandals, feeling how different they are from other footwear, sensing the lightness which the sandals give, moving over the space, taking themselves over mountains, rivers, cities and so forth, and reconnoitring over the land of the Gorgons. A similar procedure can be followed with the helmet which made him invisible, and everyone can sense the pleasure of being able to vanish, in a variety of situations.

Next, all can handle the shield on one arm and a sword in the other hand, fighting first normally with the weapons and then battling against enemies, using the shield as a mirror.

At this point each member of the group can go back to the beginning of the story and tell it slowly through, adding further items of adventure as everyone acts out the journey to the Gorgons, the killing, and the return.

In a similar way, everyone can be a Gorgon, using arms to represent snakes. Some can imagine that their heads are cut off by Perseus, others can pursue him when they see Medusa executed. Finally, the leader can organize groups of four and let each act out the story in its own time, making its own imaginative build-up.

2. WITH A DELINQUENT GROUP OF THIRTEEN-YEAR-OLDS

The group for this purpose would probably only be eight to twelve in number. Here again bring this group into a circle and start off a story, asking each member of the group to introduce another person or thing when he takes over his section of the story. Preferably, no special order should be followed, but someone could point to the person he wanted to continue the story. The story might start something like this:

"At six o clock one morning a man left his house with a suitcase in his hand . . ." The leader then points to one of the group, who might continue: "He was going to catch a train to the sea-side . . ." Another person is indicated and goes on: "As he entered the station, he dropped his suitcase and a woman in nurse's uniform rushed up and said . . ." and so on till the story has developed.

The leader could then either get the group to act out all or part of their story or explain that just as the group had a starting-point and then went on with whatever came into their heads at the moment when they had to continue the story, so he will give them a starting-point for their acting and get them to continue with whatever happens to occur to them at the time. Depending on numbers, he would be advised to divide his group into two or three smaller groups for this purpose. He might then give each group a place, a person and a thing (the same, or different ones to each group) or three objects or just one idea (a person, place or thing).

As starting-points, for instance, he might suggest one or two items like: a hen-house, an ice-lolly, a baby, an attic, a sock with a hole in it, a piece of Gorgonzola cheese, a circus clown, a public swimming-bath, a mint with a hole in the middle, and ask the group to act out a story involving these as they go along. If the group seem to find it difficult to begin, he can help them with questions one at a time, such as, How did you get there . . . in your attic? What time of day is it? Who are you? What are you wearing on your feet, your head, your hands? Whereabouts are they . . . these things you've been given? What other things are near you? What have you got in your pockets? Later, if the group can take anything more complicated, it could be suggested that they are suspicious of the other people and should try to find out all they can about the others without revealing anything about themselves.

After some time on this particular project, he can change the composition of the groups, so that individuals are working with different people. He can give them something oral to start with – like a scream, a works siren, a telephone bell, a knock at the door, an explosion, a clock ticking. His aim would be throughout the session to aid the groups to respond freely, so that whatever developed sprang spontaneously from what had just gone before and was a result of free expressive flow of ideas. These improvisations should have something of the rambling and inconclusive form that the story in the beginning showed.

3. WITH FOURTEEN–FIFTEEN-YEAR-OLDS IN A SECONDARY MODERN SCHOOL

THEME: *Teen-age World*. Begin with everyone walking around the space available as a teen-ager. Get them to be aware of teen-age clothes – jeans, sweaters, shoes and so on. Encourage them to use the space and to begin walking in different directions without knocking into anyone. Let them walk in different moods and different feelings, sometimes with enthusiasm, sometimes "couldn't care less"; then in their imaginations ask them to walk as if they were going home, and eventually imagine they had reached their house, where they could go in and put on the radio or a record. This could be repeated with different physical and mental attitudes and other occupations be introduced. Then ask them to imagine a shop to which they are going to buy a raincoat or jacket. In this preliminary work some or all of it could be done against the background of a record if it is found that the sound helps to aid release of tension. From this work in which all the individuals have been responding solo but simultaneously we might move on to work in threes, in which they take up again the buying of new clothes – shoes, gloves and so on – the groups themselves deciding who will buy and who sell, and what the identity of the third person might be. Encourage the use of speech in seeking what is required and discussing the merits of the purchase. They can then go on to change roles and lead into a credit sale. Develop this into the purchase proving unsatisfactory in some way and the buyer returning to the shop to complain.

At this point we can have a change round in groups, so that people get an opportunity of working with different individuals, and build a scene in a market in which someone is accused of stealing and a passer-by joins in on one side or the other. Encourage the group to suggest developments and explore them. Let them discover the difference between being accused of stealing when the person has stolen something and when he has not. Introduce a further element in which the law, or some other authority, is involved in the scene. Depending on time and response, the leader can afford the opportunity for everyone to experience the different roles, and some chance of a further change in the constitution of the group. Allow the groups time for discussion of details and rehearsals, so that they try to get things to their satisfaction. In rehearsal periods it is as well to give a clear indication that they have, say, a couple of minutes only before they will be asked to run through the scene as far as they have been able to develop it.

4. ALTERNATIVE SESSION FOR FOURTEEN–FIFTEEN-YEAR-OLDS INVOLVING A MORE IMAGINATIVE WORLD

THEME: *Western Saloon.* The approach is similar, but instead of teen-agers in their own town, they imagine themselves as cowboys walking, leaping, aware of the difference of clothing, holsters, engaging in occupations like seeing to the horses, walking through the swing doors of the saloon, talking at the bar counter, buying a drink. Then in threes go on to card playing with an argument breaking out over cheating, songs round the piano, introducing the sheriff, rehearsing a gun fight. Finally, get the group to build a scene involving the mood of the saloon, its music, drinks, card playing. The stranger enters, there is an argument, a gun fight, and the sheriff's arrival. Encourage the group to talk in their improvisations if this helps them to overcome their self-consciousness.

Younger groups usually demand much more obvious activity than older ones and like to build their work round life's more forceful moments, such as accidents, escapes, fires, killing, robbery, death and shipwrecks.

5. WITH A GROUP OF FAIRLY EXPERIENCED ACTORS WHO HAVE NOT DONE MUCH IMPROVISATION BEFORE

THEME: *World of the theatre.* The first five minutes might be spent in gaining flexibility based upon the various muscle groups. There can be some regular physical exercise for each part of the body, leading in to an imaginative expression which will involve fairly free use of each part of the body. Then some music could be played and the group given opportunity for free movement or dance expression.

Depending on the imaginative response, the leader might help the group to extend their range of response to the music by stopping at different points and asking the actors to move or dance in less usual ways. He might ask them to dance with other parts of the body, the head alone, the hips, the shoulders, or he can ask them to pay special attention to the space behind them or at the side, above or below them, or he might ask them to cover more of the space in their movement, or to dance in unusual ways, such as bent double, with one hand touching the floor, leaping into the air and so on.

In the last few moments of the music they can be asked to

imagine that they are getting ready for an audition. Let them work
in threes on a scene in which they find themselves waiting to be
auditioned. Groups can develop their own scene, which might be
simply the three meeting and beginning to talk, exchanging their
different responses in anticipation of meeting the casting director.
They may be called and return one by one with appropriate comments, or an incident may develop in which someone faints or gets
excited. From this, each of them goes to his home and enjoys some
relaxation. Afterwards, the phone rings and the message proves to
be an offer of a contract. Repeat this individually, in pairs, and in
threes, taking it in turns to share the news and the experience.
Encourage the groups to avoid making any obvious response and
get them to work instead on improving the imaginative reality.

This can lead into work with larger groups or smaller scenes
building into one, incorporating everyone. Work on a scene in
which one person in the group has good news and the others join
in a party of celebration. Again, give opportunity for revision and
try to help individuals, to avoid any kind of cliché response. Call
for only those reactions which are honestly felt. Finally, discuss
with the group a scene which could be built using all the elements
which have been experienced throughout the session. Give time
and opportunity for rehearsal and a final run-through.

In any session it is vital to proceed with clarity step by step. At
any one time give only enough instruction to enable everyone to
get on with the work. Ensure that everyone is confident in carrying
out the small exercises before proceeding to the longer scenes.

Some general points about making a start

We have outlined only five possible first sessions. There are, of
course, many other ways of approaching a first session, and ideas
put forward in later chapters will suggest other ways of organizing
an introductory meeting. Of the five suggested, these are not
suitable only for the age range mentioned, nor is the material
applicable only to that kind of group. The material outlined could
be used with any group, provided that it is rearranged and presented in a manner suitable to the age and experience of those
taking part.

It is from these first sessions that the leader will select points of
focus for his later improvisation work. He may choose to proceed

from smaller exercises to more involved work, or he may feel it is more suitable for his group to work within a given dramatic framework and select from this shorter sections on which to develop the concentration, spontaneity, imagination and so on with his group. Chapter 11 suggests ways in which a play may be built from improvisation, and some may like to use some of the ideas put forward there to form the basis for developing the programme.

Assessing the first session

Right from the start improvisations should be raising questions in the minds of those taking part. They should also be raising questions in the leader's mind. He will be noticing those who respond easily, and will be asking himself why. He will be noticing those who found it difficult or impossible to respond easily and he will again be looking for the reasons. Which part of the session seemed to bring greatest concentration? Do they seem easiest working on a physical level, talking, using real props or imaginary, or what combination of any of these? Which people seemed most difficult for others to work with, and why? Which people seemed to draw others into absorption quickly? Was the material always suitable? Was my approach to the material right for the group? Did I try to do too much or too little? What is the most obvious need for focus next time?

This is the sort of problem he might be putting to himself, and without expecting to find the answers to all, such pointers will help to tune his awareness.

Loosening-up activities

These might come at any point in the session, depending on the aim and structure of the work. At some point, however, it is useful to prepare those taking part through some loosening-up activity focused specially on the body, the voice and the imagination. Wherever possible, this training should be linked in its imaginative presentation with the other work planned, and will flow into the other activities naturally. Again, depending on how the session is organized, these activities might be taken one following another, or linked, or given at different points throughout the session. Here are some general ideas and considerations.

a] physical – designed to free and exercise all parts of the body. Sometimes it may be no more than a general shaking out of hands, feet, head and shoulders, trunk, midriff and legs. At other times, after some general activity such as walking, running, jumping, skipping and so on, we might lead into focusing attention on one or two aspects of the body – hands and arms, or legs and feet, or head and shoulders, or trunk. With more advanced groups we can spent time in concentrating simply upon details such as fingers or facial expression.

b] imaginative – this involves the use we make of the body and would lead in the first sessions into discovery of the body in space, different ways of using space, different kinds of space, and so on. Similarly, with an imaginative exploration of weight, moving with lightness and heaviness, moving against resistance, or being driven along by something, and the imaginative use of time, the rate at which we move. Each of these will lead to combining with the other two in an imaginative way, for instance, using the body with lightness and slowness, or slowly against resistance. A further dimension can be added by taking our imaginative use of combined weight, space and time into an occupation such as pushing a piano, throwing a ball, catching a bubble. Laban's classification of efforts in *Modern Educational Dance* (Macdonald and Evans) (wring, press, glide, float, flick, slash, dab, punch) with help to stimulate imagination further and can be followed through in all kinds of situations. Groups can be encouraged both to discover as many different ways as possible of using weight, space and time (e.g. moving near the floor, high in the air, forwards, backwards, sideways, crawling, rolling, leaping, twisting, twirling) and of finding as many different occupations as they can which employ the effort qualities (e.g. flicking which is employed in knocking dust from the body with the hands, kicking away a spider or unpleasant object, shivering with cold). Various movement games can be used in which, say, the group move around freely either to music or without, and at a given signal are asked to hold whatever position the body happens to be in. This position they are then asked to use as an imaginative start for some occupation.

c] vocal – aimed to release and tune up the voice. We could begin by making vocal sounds, concentrating at times upon agility and flexibility or the parts of the mouth employed in speaking. At other times we can work more on kinds and qualities of sound. From the making of simple sounds we can move into the building of words, phrases, sentences and the development of richness and subtlety of expression. We can discover also how different qualities of voice and kinds of speech vary with different movement patterns. All this vocal work can be linked with imaginative work, and ensures each session that the vocal instrument and its link with the imagination is prepared for the rest of the work in the session.

Music is a useful aid and stimulus in all this early work and can be used to aid the group to respond to its mood or to start the imagination working. In early sessions the group would probably move as individuals and, as time went on, small groups might form, while at some points everyone might find themselves coming together in the building of one movement pattern. The type of music used should be varied from session to session, using classical, jazz, swing, pop, "modern classical" or simply percussion.

Developing improvisation

There is certain to be plenty of variation in the subject-matter of the work and we need to keep a variety in the method of approach. The other important thing is to ensure that there is a sense of progression from one session to the next and that the standard of work shows a gradual improvement. This can be aided by giving groups direct points on which to work (according to the overall plan) and reminding them during the time they have for rehearsal of projects to ensure that they have achieved the aim with clarity. With time, we can look for greater penetration and understanding in discussion, and later, when they begin to watch each other's work, we can encourage good observation and insight in their comments. At times, after discussion, groups can be asked to work again on the same scenes, trying this time to correct the main faults or improve generally the clarity of expression and interest.

As a variation of the approach in which the main group is divided into small groups and given an assignment, we might start off someone in one part of the room with an activity, getting others to join them at differing intervals of time. Speech can be used as and when desirable. Other groups can begin in a different part of the room in a similar way, and develop this until scenes evolve. Then can follow a discussion of the scenes in which the qualities and atmospheres, as well as the truth of the group work, are talked about. Individuals will usually be interested to comment on what movement or speech pattern sparked off the ideas and how development took place. The scenes can be developed either by working on them again after this discussion or by building the various scenes and ideas into a single improvisation.

Another useful approach is in setting the groups a particular problem associated with the aim of the session; for example, they might be asked to consider what makes a good entrance, and then they` could be given time to talk about it in their small groups, afterwards being asked to build a scene illustrating an effective entrance and an ineffectual entrance.

Sometimes when the work is becoming more advanced it may be as well to think in terms of a two-session development, so that the second meeting could be devoted to longer periods of work. This has also the value of giving time for the maturing of ideas and exploration and research away from the acting area. In all the work it is as well to ensure that in small groups ample opportunity is given for work with different people, so that individuals can appreciate the different demands and responses needed with different people. Keep in mind also the need for each session to add up to something, and the more the work develops the clearer the aim should appear (even when we might fall short of it), and the less sessions should appear a succession of unrelated scenes and situations.

SHARING

When some absorption in improvised work has been achieved the work in small groups can be shared with those in the other groups. The best atmosphere is achieved by avoiding any suggestion of performance, in the spirit of "Let's have a look at this group and see how far they have been able to get". If groups are working in various parts of the same room, it is easiest to ask them to act their improvisation where they have been working.

Most groups, especially inexperienced ones, will need some guidance on what to look for when sharing another group's work. The leader might give two or three points for everyone to bear in mind while watching. These would depend on the aim of the particular session. If, for instance, the aim was to develop imagination, those looking on might be asked to observe inventiveness, both visual and oral, and effectiveness of execution. After the improvisations had been given, the leader could then draw from the group both what they liked and why, and what improvements they thought could be made and why. Again, there can be some variety in the ways in which sharing is carried out. It is not always necessary to have the questions after each group has shown its work, and the number and variety of questions will depend on the aim and amount of development desired. Sometimes the discussion can be left till all improvisations have been seen and general comments, with examples, can be made. Similarly, sometimes a sampling of the work will be more helpful, especially if different groups are looked at at different times.

IMPROVISATION IN A LIMITED SPACE WITH HEAVY FURNITURE

As we have already suggested, limited space means a limitation in the improvisation, but it need not discourage leaders altogether from attempting this work, while they are agitating for more ideal conditions. Ingenuity is required and a certain selectivity is necessary. The introductory work will need to be designed to give what movement activity is practicable. If necessary, this may have to be confined to trunk, head and arm movements. If a leader is having to work with groups in a room where, say, there are some very heavy desks, he could arrange work on an individual level and in pairs without a great deal of difficulty. Then, with a little more care and planning, groups of three and four can be organized. Sometimes, instead of regarding the furniture merely as an obstacle, it can be involved in the activity, so that people can sit on it, stand on it, lean on it, move round it, over it, under it, and use imaginative ingenuity in making it become something else.

Where noise is likely to cause annoyance to other people, some of the work can be arranged so as to keep the vocal power used to a minimum. Discussion would then need to be handled with very little vocalizing of the sound, that is, almost whispering. With some age groups, the imaginative element can be utilized to suggest, say, the need for secrecy, or another arrangement might be made so that in a group of, for instance thirty, ten only could be using sound, while the others worked in mime or whispers.

In this kind of work, where noise and space are limited, it is still important to avoid any suggestion of performance and working "out in front". It is better still to share work from the point at which it has been carried out, even though this may mean slight regrouping of the rest of the people in the room.

Because drama is working with the whole person, activity both physical and vocal is essential. Though it is possible to carry on with severe limitations, it has to be reiterated that this does mean a limitation of the work also.

CHAPTER 5

Developing Concentration and Spontaneity

Concentration is the key to overcoming nervousness and anxiety about other people and what they will think. With this development we train interest and absorption, both of which are essential for creativity at its fullest and the quality of truth demanded. In the present-day world we are constantly affected by increasing distractions, conspiring against concentration. We become familar with ever-increasing noise, which has its manifestations in the fact that the world of pop seems to be becoming louder and louder. Sounds of one sort or another are constantly in the background. We even become afraid of silence. Similarly, we are constantly having demands made on our eyes: large hoardings, advertisements on cinema and television screens, picture newspapers, vast headlines and so on. All this means that we look and listen with less attentiveness, and this in its turn means decreasing human efficiency. From the more direct point of view of acting, concentration is essential to the sustaining of any kind of characterization, situation or mood, and lack of concentration at other times means living a shallower existence.

Throughout this training, concentration needs to be developed both with the whole person and with the focus being placed from time to time on concentration with specific senses. A planned approach to concentration might develop on these lines:

(i) *Looking* – concentration on what we see, and observation of detail.

(ii) *Listening* – concentration on what is heard and qualities of meaning in sound.

(iii) *Touching* – concentration on feeling things: size, texture and so on.

(iv) *Seeing and touching* – working on the co-ordination of these senses.

(v) *Smelling* – concentration on kinds and qualities.

(vi) *Tasting* – concentration on kinds and qualities.

Throughout the aim should be to train concentration and

observation in relation to meaning and not just isolated memory. When some kind of understanding of shape is discernible the rote memory factor is reduced and observation is seen to have a purpose. Usually we shall work from observation of, and concentration on, first things and then people.

FROM OBSERVATION TO CONCENTRATION

i] *Looking*

Here are some ways of developing observation and concentration with the eyes:

> look around the room at straight lines;
> look around the room at squares;
> look around the room at circles.

Notice ways in which these are combined in different objects:

> look at a collection of objects found in the kitchen – say fifteen – for about a minute, and see how many you can bring into a short scene: notice how they combine straight lines, squares and circles;
>
> look at a photograph or picture of a scene or action for about a minute, then build an improvisation, using as much of the detail as you can;
>
> look at the clothing someone is wearing, then imagine you are packing a suitcase with all these items in it;
>
> watch someone carrying out an occupation, then see if you can go through the same occupation, leaving nothing out and putting nothing new in: putting up a deck chair, to sit and read a paper, making a special cocktail, or mixing a pudding, threading an electric sewing machine, getting into a car or on to a motor bicycle and driving away;
>
> watch a machine in motion and then aim to build a faithful movement representation: inside an alarm clock, a tape recorder, a vacuum cleaner;
>
> observe someone making or assembling an object and then, separately or combined, represent the human action and the machine action: making a chair, sewing a suit.

Then on to more detailed concentration on people:

look at people running, walking, dancing: concentrate on movement lines: reproduce these separately and in scenes;

look at expressions on the face and attempt to re-create these: use a mirror to check on your results;

get some members of the group to adopt a disguise: notice the detail of this;

observe the effect of light on the body, changing shape, expression and so on: build scenes in which people are sitting in different lights, leading to mistaken identity or change of expression, mood and so on;

notice different movement patterns with different ages – from baby to grandad, different bearings of different occupations, different social conditions, and employ these scenes as accurately as possible.

Work in pairs, one performing actions, the other responding as the mirror image.

ii] *Listening*

Listen to various sounds, recorded or live.

Aim to reproduce these: (*a*) using any materials to hand, (*b*) with the voice: door-bell, hooter, creaking boards, lighting the gas: use these in short scenes either with one person making the sound and the other person making the action, or with both operations carried out by the same person;

hear a short tune or musical phrase whistled, sung or played and attempt to re-create it: try again with longer and more complicated pieces: build a scene round a repeated tune, i.e. where a snatch of tune is an important part of the plot or the tune acts as a backing to the action;

listen to the rhythm of an engine or piece of apparatus and build on this, making an interesting sound pattern which might be expressed in movement or dramatic terms;

listen to a piece of music: capture its rhythmic patterns and repeat these, with the voice and any other means of percussion;

listen to different kinds of voices and try to mimic these in a scene: notice different expressions and devise scenes to bring out changes in meaning;

classify sounds, observing long and short, staccato, sustained, harsh and smooth and so on, and use the effects each has to heighten or support the mood of a scene;

correlate human and non-human sounds and work on scenes bringing out parallels and contrasts;

listen to a sound, such as a knock on the door, or thunder, or a brass band and respond to the sound, trying to ensure that the response is an inner and true one: build a scene round this;

in groups all concentrate on one sound and build a group scene from a group reaction;

use a real or imaginary radio or record player to bring different human responses to the varying musical extracts or voices or languages;

listen to someone at the other end of a telephone;

respond to a street-corner orator or political speaker;

listen to the nagging of a mother, father, husband or wife: in each case, respond as an individual or a group.

iii] *Touching*

Feel objects of varying size and shape:

with eyes closed, or blindfolded, touch the same objects and then move on to others;

create scenes in which someone who is blind has to identify something by its touch;

feel the different textures of fabrics, the different surfaces of wood, metal, stone, etc.: touch these with parts of the body other than the hands and see if you can recognize the same object;

work next on the weight of objects, relating these to size and shape;

work on the touch of liquids of varying viscosity, noticing the different sensations these have to the skin of face, hands, feet, etc.;

next, move on to the touch of things over the skin, the different feeling of various kinds of gloves, those with fingers, without fingers, with half-fingers, different materials, leather, wool, lace, cotton, gloves which end at the wrist, continue up the arm, gauntlets;

feel different kinds of footwear – slippers, low-heeled shoes, high-heeled shoes, sandals, boots, thigh-boots;

feel footwear from different periods and countries;

build some of these as the focal point of a scene;

work also on the feeling of heat and cold, both extreme and more temperate: develop this into severity of heat or cold to one part of the body and experience the pain resulting;

explore sensations of pleasure arising from sense of touch, such as clean sheets, a warm muff, a hot-water bottle, the sun, the rain, and so on;

next, work on physical touch between people: groups will need to be encouraged to overcome fears of touching people: begin with the touch which draws attention to something: a tap on the shoulder, prod in the back, kick of the foot: then go on to the touch of comfort or aggression;

explore the touch involved in handling a wounded leg, a baby, a delicate object.

Again, all or some of these can be worked into scenes.

iv] *Seeing and touching*

We can now go on to building scenes in which sight plays an important part alongside touch:

work in pairs in handling an imaginary object, such as a banana, a cigarette, a cup of tea, and then pass it to another person, aiming to keep aware of the reality of size, shape, texture, etc.; these can be developed into scenes in which the object is imagined, but in which we concentrate upon the three-dimensional quality – its size, shape, texture and its colour.

Occupations involving people and things can help in the further development of concentration with these combined senses:

repairing a puncture, cleaning out a caravan, dealing with a burst pipe, making pastry, doing a home perm.

At different stages, we can concentrate our attention solely upon one area of the body, and it is useful all through the work to narrow down our focus at times into the special observation, imagination and expressiveness of:

hands and arms,
feet and legs,

face, head and shoulders,
the trunk of the body.

Much of this work can be built into larger scenes such as:

jungle episodes, scenes built on science fiction (where all
sorts of strange nets and fluids can descend), underground
scenes involving caves and passages and obstacles, or simply
scenes which involve removals in a house with many staircases
and awkward rooms. Improvised speech can be introduced at
any stage of this work on concentration and sound effects made
both by the group acting, or by another group, will add variety.

v] *Smelling*

If possible, start with actual smells – bottled or produced on the
spot, and work on to imagining these.

Identify a series of smells or perfumes, roses, violets, hock, hay,
dinner cooking (or burning).

Go on to exploration in, say, a park where a scene can be built
involving the various perfumes which are about.

Next, take the opposite and be in a dank underground area
where we can identify rotting vegetation and various gases. These
can be explored in relation not only to their unpleasantness but
also to their choking quality and their effect on health.

A scene can then be worked on, in which two contrasting smells
play an important part in the action.

Explore the ideas that certain towns or districts have their own
smell and its associative link with nostalgia.

vi] *Tasting*

Again, if possible, concentrate on actual tastes – small pieces of
different kinds of chocolate to be identified, different drinks,
alcoholic and otherwise, different brands, say, of coffee, or kinds
of tea – Indian or China – and devise scenes to employ some of
these.

Imagine other tastes and attempt some kind of classification –
bitter, sour (discuss the difference between these two), sweet, dry,
wet, hot, cold.

Work on the reality of different flavours and explore the relationship between taste and touch in the mouth, noting the texture which drink and foods have. Many ideas for scenes will rise from this work.

All this work can build into concentration on a combination of one or two or more of the senses.

MORE DIFFICULT CONCENTRATION PRACTICE

As groups find it easier to concentrate upon one or more factors, we can introduce elements of distraction and situations like the following can be devised to help sustain the absorption:

one person in a group starts whistling a tune, is joined by a second whistling another tune, then by a third, and so on: each aims to maintain his own tune without increasing the volume;

whistling tunes as above, and while keeping one's own tune going, try to recognize as many of the other tunes as possible;

read a newspaper article aloud, as various people try to interrupt one's train of thought;

read a simple story aloud, with interruptions from others: this time, when anyone interrupts the reader, he keeps his finger on the spot reached, listens to the interrupter, answers him, and continues with the story to the next interruption, and so on to the end of the story, seeing how clearly he can maintain his own concentration;

deliver a speech, being heckled by many people: maintain the line of argument without being ruffled by any of the shouts from the floor;

deliver an argument answering hecklers who should always derive their interruptions from the speech while attempting to draw red herrings: answer these interruptions calmly, return each time to the main line of argument;

an object, say a pen, is placed in view on a table or in a jacket pocket; one character tries to take this while distracting the other person's concentration;

repeat the above exercise, trying to do it more and more openly and with less attempt at tricking the other person;

establish a character of a different nationality from your own, and try to sustain this while meeting characters from other situations: the aim should be to be able to meet other characters and respond to them in character without losing identity;

play a character in a particular style – say, Restoration or Victorian, and find yourself in a world quite different: see how much detail of character can be sustained;

see if you can get a character who is carrying gloves to leave them behind without realizing.

SPONTANEITY

The more spontaneity which has been achieved in the work so far, the better the improvisations that are likely to develop. From time to time, special attention can be given to trying to improve spontaneity. Students should be encouraged to avoid censoring their responses, or planning their actions ahead. This is linked a good deal with their absorption for the more they can become preoccupied with what is happening the easier it is for them to meet the situation naturally and frankly. The following are some of the differing approaches which might be made in developing spontaneity:

simple stream-of-consciousness techniques: a word is said by one member of a small group and each member of the group in turn responds immediately with another word to whatever word has just been uttered;

a story is begun and continued in a similar manner to the one suggested at the start of the session on page 38;

in small groups, one member begins putting an imaginary object inside a suitcase: he is joined by another member who takes the suitcase and takes out a quite different object, handing it to the third member who packs something again quite different: this can be done with or without words, but the aim is always to let the previous object suggest the subsequent response;

telling a story: in pairs passing the narrative from one to the other;

in groups, this time at the end of each section or narrative, before passing on to the next person, one member of the group asks either how, or when, or why or where for the next person to respond to;

take an article of clothing and wear it, passing it on in a scene to another member of the group, making it change its function each time;

in pairs, take it in turns to move: each movement is stimulated by whatever movement has been made by the previous person;

start inventing something practical and let it develop into as many other things as you can, each thing growing out of the previous one;

do the same, working in pairs or threes;

set groups working on scenes separately and then bring two of the scenes together and let them respond to the new situation as spontaneously as they can;

again set scenes going and introduce a new element at any point, e.g. the ceiling is beginning to lower, a telegram arrives, some men start taking your furniture away, your trousers are beginning to fall down, the temperature has dropped forty degrees, your environment has completely changed to a desert island, the moon, a molehill.

SPONTANEITY AND SCRIPTED DRAMA

For spontaneity a complete lack of tension is essential, and each time the leader notices that tension is returning he may find it useful to come back to spontaneity exercises. Tension seems to build particularly rapidly when many people find themselves with the script of a play in their hands. Free open thought tends to be blocked, and when leaders find this happening it is vital to encourage actors to put down the scripts and improvise on the ideas which lie behind the words. Actors can be reminded of this work and, in other improvisations linked with the script, helped to realize that the response they are now working on is the total result of listening to and seeing all that has just been said or done by other actors, and that what they must avoid is a kind of reflex trained to go into action at a given word or sign.

CHAPTER 6

Stimulating the Imagination

With imagination we can surmount any conditions or circumstances. "I could be bounded in a nutshell and count myself King of infinite space." If, at the same time, we had the courage to use our imagination, it is possible that we could overcome many of the circumstances which usually overcome us. Apart from the need we have for imagination in making progress in industry and the home, it is also important on the more purely human level. In this way we can gain insight into other people, grasp patterns of relationships and see the link between people and things.

It is clear that while we have been working to gain increased concentration we have also been involving and extending the imagination. But now we shall direct our attention to ways of developing still further the many aspects of our imagination. This work will be greatly facilitated if a good degree of concentration has been acquired by this stage. Each of the senses which we explored in our development of concentration will suggest useful starting-points for stimulation of the imagination.

Each stimulus to the imagination can be used in this kind of development:

a] Experiencing.
b] Reproducing or describing it.
c] Linking it with other things, either an immediate free-association or looking around or discussion of links.
d] Using the findings to build up a scene or scenes.

The overall pattern of the work will follow this kind of progression:

1. Imaginative work building from observation of real things and people (either making them imaginatively real or using them imaginatively).
2. Go on to adding insight and experience to discover further ways of using the real and imaginary elements.

3. Build something new from the imagination, based on insight into, and experience of the old, leading on to –
4. Realizing the limitless bounds of the imagination.

Here are some examples of ways in which these principles might be worked out:

I. BUILDING FROM OBSERVATION

Look at and handle a football, a hat, a guitar, a passport, a parcel; in turn, remove the object and look at, and handle, each in the imagination;

work the arm of a gramophone, plane a piece of wood, repair a light fuse, then perform each with the imaginary objects;

watch a girl skipping, a boy blowing up a Lilo, a lady looking for something in her handbag;

perform the same actions accurately, using imaginary objects; work in pairs and small groups and check each other's imaginative accuracy;

describe an actual route to someone and see if they can then conduct you along it in an imaginative scene;

prepare a diagram of the centre of your nearest city; explain its layout to someone, and see if then they can take you on a conducted tour of the area in the imagination;

draw a plan of the layout of your house from the memory in your imagination, and check it with reality;

describe to someone where an object is to be found in a nearby room and see if your imaginative description is accurate enough to help them find the object;

look at a film-strip; see if you can recall the order and contents of the frames, seeing each clearly in your imagination;

look at some short excerpts of film; re-imagine the sequence, describing it as you go along;

listen to an actual gramophone record of:

pop-music
classical music
dog bark
church bells;

see if you can recall each clearly in imagination, first immediately after listening to the sound and then when some other sound intervenes between the first item listened to and the imaginative recall;

drink a small quantity of orange juice, lemon juice, vinegar, cold tea, and then see if you can recall accurately the taste;

smell some mint or other herbs, and recall them vividly in imagination;

give one or more imaginary objects, such as a telescope, a bird cage, a book of trading stamps, or give a place, such as a deserted house, an underground railway station, and use them to build a scene;

have a variety of hats (soldier's cap, policeman's helmet, wedding veil, floral hat) and distributing one or two to a group, build a scene.

2. OBSERVATION WITH INSIGHT AND EXPERIENCE

Take a chair or similar object, sit on it in as many different ways as you can devise; explore other possibilities, such as ways of standing on it, or moving round it;

take a small table or desk (or the chair again); look at it from different points of view, turn it on its side, upside down, and treat it as something else: a windshield, book rest, shelter;

take other objects, such as a shoe, book, pen, ring; find as many ways as you can of using each;

treat each as something else;

work on the real and the imagined objects;

imagine an object, such as a vacuum cleaner; use it; then endow it with another quality, such as the ability to light the fire;

or an electric fire which talks;

or a standard lamp which has certain human attributes;

imagine a dog or other animal which you train from its animal noise into words of speech;

imagine the shop of a trade or occupation such as shoe repairing, or dry cleaning, where the objects bring with them certain associations of, or for, the people who own them.

take several of these ideas, introduce an element of tension or conflict, and develop into scenes.

3. NEW IDEAS FROM OLD

Act out a situation in which mother, father, son and daughter have changed roles;

take some characters from a book recently read; act out a situation in which they come to life and look at the fiction of the present day;

put three people in a strange situation such as waking up to find themselves in a sea-side hotel, unable to remember how they got there and let the situation develop;

take over an imaginary house, barn, windmill or oasthouse, and set about alterations and improvements from your imagination;

build scenes around the idea of tricks of the imagination: shapes in the night seeming like other shapes, noises in the fog seeming to come from different directions and to mean different things, or seeing one person as another, in a state of intoxication;

imagine a character or characters with an oversensitive sense of smell and a strong imagination, or strong senses of taste and imaginations which run away with them; develop scenes and situations from these;

given an imaginary £50, act out a scene in which you spend it, or lose it or give it away;

in a world of the blind, imagine being misled by misinterpreting items of touch and hearing.

4. IMAGINATION WITHOUT BOUNDS

Devise scenes in which all the characters except one are: (i) deaf, (ii) unable to speak, (iii) without taste, (iv) blind; imagine this handicap affecting the whole way of living – new design of things used, new standards of judgement (cf. *Country of the Blind*, by H. G. Wells);

imagine a world in which everyone is (i) very, very small, (ii) tall, (iii) heavy, (iv) lighter than air; imaginatively explore this change of situation (cf. *The Truth about Pyecraft*, by H. G. Wells);

build scenes around eccentric people who are always imagining that they have people in the room or who imagine that the whole situation around them is different from what it is;

    work out scenes in which characters from one period of history find themselves in another period, or people from one country or civilization find themselves suddenly placed in another;

    imagine a world in which language has been lost, and a new one has to be invented;

    imagine a hundred years hence, and the people of that time discovering some of the sealed containers full of objects typical of our age, and their reactions to them;

    starting from some ideas from Samuel Butler's *Erewhon*, build scenes in a world where everything is the opposite of what it is in this world (where men are punished for being ill, and put into hospital for committing a crime).

Happenings

All improvisations are, to some extent, happenings in the sense that none of the participants is exactly sure what is going to happen. As we have already discussed, this is linked with the quality of spontaneity which is one of the elements we have been aiming to develop.

For the British theatre, however, at the Edinburgh Festival 1963, the word "happening" took on a more particularized meaning at the Drama Conference. This is how Ken Dewey, one of the organizers of the happening, describes the event in *Encore* No. 46:

"What we set out to arrange was the gradual introduction of about fifteen elements into the conference while a discussion and debate (also planned) were in progress.

"A list of the elements, in the order in which they were intended to appear, was as follows:

    A platform speaker (Charles Marowitz) making a pseudo-serious proposal that the conference formally accept, as the definitive interpretation, his explanation of *Waiting for Godot*.
    An audience member (Charles Lewsen) attacking the speaker for being unclear and not heroic enough.
    From outside a tape of cable-pullers at work.
    Low and barely audible organ sounds.
    The silhouette of a large head at the top of the dome of the hall.

A second tape made from fragments of speeches at the conference.

A man walking the tiny ledge high up at the base of the dome.

Figures appearing at other windows high above the hall and occasionally staring down at the people.

An actress on the platform (Carrol Baker) beginning to stare at someone at the back of the hall (Allan Kaprow), eventually taking off a large fur coat and moving towards him across the tops of the audience seats.

A nude model (Anne Kesselaar) being whisked across the organ loft on a spotlight stand.

The men at the high windows (Rik Kendell and Patrick De Salvo) shouting "Me! Can you hear me? Me!"

Carrol Baker reaching Allan Kaprow, and both running out of the hall together.

Tape, organ and debate continue.

A bagpiper (Hamish MacLeod) crossing the top balcony.

A sheep skeleton hung on the giant flat with Cocteau's symbol of the conference.

The piper reaching the other end of the hall as all other sounds stopped, and a blue curtain behind the platform being dropped to reveal shelves containing about fifty white plaster death masks (or, to be more precise, phrenological head studies).

A woman with a baby, and a boy with a radio entering the hall, mounting the platform, looking at everything as if in a museum, and leaving. The piper tapering off in the distance.

(Running time of the piece was calculated as seven minutes.)

"The piece was intended as a surprise, to be introduced without prior comment. However, through some mistake, it was announced. Feeling angry enough to call the whole thing off, I gave a premature cue which sent the nude and several other elements on their way very near the beginning. As it worked out this was the perfect accident to offset whatever expectations the announcement might have generated in the audience. Where a slow build would have been the right tempo for a situation in which nothing was expected, a quick surprise was better suited for an audience that was waiting to be 'shown'. It is not unusual for change, accident, or unusual circumstances to supply such a piece with its most appropriate rhythm."

The purpose of this happening was to animate a conference which to many people seemed dull and divorced from vital communication. The apparently unrelated incidents attempt to make their own comment on the overintellectualized rarefied atmosphere. The purpose of all this seems to have been to try to shock the audience from its complacency. From the actors little was called for, apart from their performing the actions prescribed and rehearsed. Everything was directed at those sitting passively "in front".

To this extent, the happening achieved its purpose: the event became news and lively arguments followed, though it must be admitted that often discussion centred on the nude model rather than on drama.

The main function of any happening is to shake those present out of their pattern of set responses. Both actors and audience seek the kind of security which comes from knowing what is expected from them, and which enables them to respond quickly and safely in an appropriate way. They tend to want the kind of security which comes from rehearsing behaviour patterns, whereas a much better way would be to train general ability and flexibility in response. It is the difference between the specialist training of dog-like reflexes to the bell and the overall fitness of the athlete.*

In this book we are concerned with the value of the shock or happening to those taking part, as distinct from those watching, and its ability to stimulate imagination, resourcefulness and spontaneity.

These are the kind of things which might be done during a session to help develop these qualities:

Explain at the outset to the group that at some point in the session an unexpected happening will take place, and that when it does they should respond as they think best:

all the lights go out, during which some equipment disappears;
a stranger comes in, causing a disturbance;
someone faints and/or someone has hysterics;
one of the group moves in with decorating equipment and begins to paper or paint the place, hindering normal activities;
a series of gunshots are heard;
someone produces a £5 note which he declares he has just found.

* Charles Marowitz discusses the Value of Happenings in an article in *Plays and Players* for March 1965.

To leave things here would be to get very little more than shock and immediate response from the actors' point of view. What would be more interesting would be to discuss the various responses and reactions and see if, on a repetition of the occurrence, the same reaction can be set in motion with the same degree of "truth". In some instances, where a scene naturally followed, it could be interesting to work on this, either at the time or later, developing it imaginatively.

Perhaps more interesting still would be to take the happening as a basis for comedy, letting the shock this time arouse the audience's laughter: the incongruity of two quite different worlds suddenly coming together and the actors' response to this. Some of the exercises suggested in Chapter 5 on page 56 on Spontaneity, and the above exercises could be repeated for their comic effect. It will be found that it is the actor's willing acceptance of the situation and his participation in it which keeps the comedy alive.

CHAPTER 7

Dramatic Shaping and Communication

During the early stages of encouraging concentration and imaginative flow it is as well not to worry the group too much with matters of shaping and communication. But once confidence is beginning to develop, some further form in the work will be needed. The work in previous chapters has aimed to develop the basic skills of improvisation and acting and those taking part will soon begin to feel that they are anxious to give their improvised work more organization and shaping. Even before they concern themselves with sharing their work with an audience (whether this be made up of other groups or spectators from outside) they will wish to clarify and sharpen the communication amongst themselves. Each actor is communicating with the other actors in an improvisation and he will feel it necessary to develop the skill of projecting himself, his ideas, the character portrayed, the mood, and the action. Then, as the smaller groups begin to share their work with the others, there will be a desire for an increasing standard of clarity and precision.

With inexperienced yet enthusiastic groups two of the first difficulties will be that many characters speak at the same time, or some personalities tend to monopolize the situation to the exclusion of others.

To help overcome the first difficulty (that of all speaking at the same time) awareness of the problem is the first step. This can often be best realized by groups themselves in watching the work of other groups. The fault is, in fact, due partly to nervousness, and with greater confidence will probably be eased, but the other requirement is to listen as well as talk and to respond to the needs of others. Set scenes in threes where everyone has to make himself known to the other two. Scenes of investigation are also useful, whereby other characters need to know details of the situation in order to proceed. In turn, let each of the three act as host or chairman and aim to keep the others talking in turn in an evenly balanced conversation.

This latter example will also help to deal with the second problem (one person monopolizing the situation to the exclusion of others), and other ways which will help will be scenes where each in turn becomes the silent, mysterious one making some final pronouncement, only after the others have revealed the situation; scenes such as those found in modern drama, where words are used economically and pauses have meaning, can also be used.

Other early faults lie in the shaping of the improvisations. At first improvisations tend either to fade out before they have gone very far or keep going without knowing where to end. In both cases groups may need some guidance on the building of their scenes. They can be encouraged to find yardsticks of general agreement from and to which they can work in their improvised flow. Give exercises at this stage which have about four major points around which a scene can be built; for instance:

i] a young man brings his girl home to meet another member of the family;
ii] the girl discovers that she knows the house, but cannot remember its association;
iii] they show photos of a recent holiday during which the girl remembers the association, which she refuses to talk about;
iv] an ending which the group decide on their own.

Other elements of shaping to which attention needs to be drawn:

1, the beginning;
2, the ending.

Very often groups can draw upon their own experience of film, television, radio, novel, theatre, to discover different ways of beginning, and exercises can be given based on these, but the following will perhaps be some guide:

1. BEGINNINGS

i] by some definite action, for instance, a stone is hurled ·through a window, breaking the glass and landing in the middle of the playing area;
ii] by establishing a mood, for example, Mick sitting on the bed at the start of *The Caretaker*;
iii] by the entry of a chorus figure, who introduces the scene, as for instance Flim in *The Sport of my Mad Mother* by Ann Jellicoe;

iv] by the central character unfolding his own aims to the audience, for example, Richard III;

v] by minor characters introducing the situation in dialogue between them, for instance, the start of *The Wild Duck*;

vi] by a crowd rushing into the playing area, for example in *Coriolanus*;

vii] by starting with silence in an empty acting area;

viii] by starting in an empty acting area, with sounds in the distance, as in *The Long and the Short and the Tall*;

ix] by the middle of the plot being unfolded first;

x] by the end of the plot being unfolded first;

xi] by the audience being involved in the action, as in *Cockpit* by Bridget Boland.

2. ENDINGS

i] a gradual slow building to a tying up of ends, or unravelling of problems;

ii] a quick surprise ending;

iii] a mid-air ending: an ending that is no ending at all;

iv] a dramatic ending, for instance, Solness falling to his death in *The Master Builder*;

v] an ending that takes you back to the beginning, as in *The Bald Prima Donna*;

vi] by filling a stage which was completely empty at the start of the play, as in *The New Tenant* by Ionesco;

vii] by emptying a stage which was full at the start of the play;

viii] by preparing the audience for one kind of ending, then suddenly switching to another, as in *The Lark* by Anouilh;

ix] by a chorus figure bringing the play to a close, as in *A Resounding Tinkle* by N. F. Simpson;

x] by reasserting the living force when the emphasis has been on the deaths of the main characters, as in most Shakespearean tragedies;

xi] by an actor breaking the action to point a moral, as in *The Good Person of Szechwan* by Brecht.

Visual communication

Drama makes its impact not only through what is heard, nor only by looking at the people who are speaking and acting, but by seeing them in relation to each other and to the place in which acting is being carried out. Very soon groups working with improvisation develop a sense for the visual impact without any formal approach to "stage technique". The stress we are placing here is a visual reinforcement of action and situation and dialogue texture, so that communication is made on every possible level.

The main points of consideration:

1. grouping
2. levels
3. moves
4. entrances
5. exits.

I. GROUPING

Begin with a similar kind of exercise to that used in the imaginative, working on an individual placing himself in relation to an object, such as a table, a telephone or a door. Build on the observation and imagination and in small groups encourage students to comment on the different meanings obtained through bodily positions and attitudes in relation to the object.

The variety is infinite, but a few basic ideas might help as points from which to develop. Beginning with two people grouped we can see that they can be arranged close together or a varying distance apart, and that the line between them may be drawn at different angles to make different relationships with the audience.

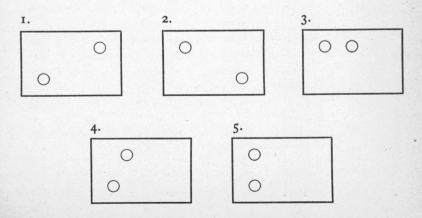

The line is given greater variety when we introduce more characters, for it can then be drawn into a circle or into a three-, four- or more-sided figure according to the number of people being used in the grouping. Clearly only sometimes will it be desirable to form a regular shape, but symmetry can be very effective in certain situations, especially those in which we wish to suggest a situation close to ritual. At other times the irregularities of the line and shape will be worked for.

In threes the triangle is especially useful as the basic shape, with many variations of apex, length of side and position of base. Here, too, there is the beginning of the circle.

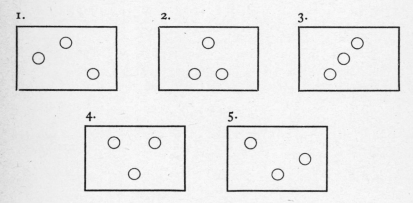

Further variety in spatial relationships will be found by the physical attitudes of the actors within the grouping, for instance, whether the actors face each other or stand with their backs to each other, trunk inclined towards or away from the centre, head turned towards or away from the centre, lunging into the centre aggressively, withdrawing from the centre in fear, and all the various changes within these ideas of two in one attitude, one in another, and each in different attitudes.

Then work with fours, fives and so into large groups and discover some of the possibilities of working with individuals and crowd to express one against the other, or for, or with, or leading, or captured by, the other and so on.

Work with people in relation to an audience placed in many different arrangements, acting near them, away from them, discovering various effects communicated by the different relation-

ships not only of the actors with other actors, but also of actors with
actors with audience.

Build these into scenes.

2. LEVELS

Continue this kind of exercise, working with different levels, first
with people standing, sitting, kneeling, using different objects.
Then go on steps or other improvised heights, experiment with
placing these fixed heights in different places in the acting area and
at all times observing different impacts and meanings which can be
conveyed. Work on to steps and platforms of different kinds, such
as pulpits, speakers' stands, public address platforms, steps of
public buildings. Move on to balconies, windows, walls, trees,
battlements, roof-tops.

Build groupings involving people on several of these levels, as
well as a group on one level against a group on another level.

Again, create scenes around these discoveries.

3. MOVES

Students will soon realize that it is very easy for improvisations
either to become static or to contain a considerable amount of
movement for its own sake. What we need to try to encourage is the
realization that, although movement does give variety and interest,
it is inextricably bound up with

   i] motivation and
   ii] meaning.

i] *Motivation:*

This is related to the actor's intent: it is his inner response to movement.

   a] Begin with students standing/sitting as individuals. Find a
   reason for sitting/standing – a knock at the door, the phone
   rings, reading a letter. Find a reason for making any movement, large or small.

   b] Work in groups. Cross to meet someone you have not seen
   for a long time.

Avoid someone you do not wish to meet.
Move to comfort somebody or to face them with bad news.

ii] *Meaning*:

That is, the communication of ideas to those watching through a
visual impact.

a] Again, begin with students standing or sitting as individuals
and ask them to find a reason for standing, running, walking
round a table, sitting on the floor. Ask them to repeat some of
these movements, but this time in such a way that the
movements they make have greater clarity and precision.
Encourage them to find a balance between the fumbled con-
cealed movement and obvious demonstration. Work on the
difference between moves which are fumbled and those
which have to appear to be so, in incidents like: stealing a
pen, buying a ring, wrapping up a parcel, mending a broken
vase.

b] In groups, work with similar aims on such incidents as:
a speaker being heckled, so that all the incidents and movements are meaningful;
a street accident, with a seriously injured person being finally
taken to hospital;
the arrival at an airport of a personality who is admired by
one section of the crowd and disliked by another.

Students also need to be led to discover that the meaning of
movements is linked with the manner. Not only does one have a
reason for moving from A to B, but this may be carried out with a
degree of speed – very slow or very fast, or any number of grada-
tions between. Also important is the degree of directness or in-
directness, as well as the quality of lightness or heaviness (Laban's
principles of time, space and weight). Link this work with the
discoveries made in the loosening-up activities (see page 43).

Any number of exercises may be devised to discover the variety of
kind and quality of movement and these can all be shaped in scenes.

4. ENTRANCES AND EXITS

These are really specific moves, but they have an additional importance and can therefore have a particular meaning and effect, so

that if badly carried out they detract from the communication. Encourage students to see that the first time a character comes into an acting space we make certain judgements about who he is and why he has come. If therefore, he does this badly, he has misled us in a more subtle way even than if he had worked through words. In this situation, it may be more difficult to put us right once he has begun to give us the wrong impression. Questions will help the student to realize that he must know why he is coming in and where he has come from.

Experiment with the position of entry, speed and directness. Similarly, when going out from a scene, ensure that the actor is going somewhere and has a reason for going.

In building entrances and exits, other characters in the scene must realize they play a part. What they have learned in grouping can be further practised here. Aim always at clarity of moving, so that even if a character must move uneasily, or enter or exit unobtrusively, the intention is clear.

CHAPTER 8

Building Characterization

The two elements we have spoken of as being basic to acting, namely impersonation and interpretation, will both be called upon and developed in characterization. The actor, unlike every other artist, ultimately creates only from himself. The musician has an instrument, the sculptor his material, but the actor is his own instrument and material. In creating a character, one has to draw upon mental, physical and emotional aspects of oneself, and as these are expressed within oneself so we convey a character. There has been a tendency in the past for character to be associated with an English tradition of stiff upper lip, straight back and inexpressive countenance – the stalwart product of the public school. For a long time in the old British sense to have character was not to show any.

In improvisation the opposite is what is being called for, for the actor is being trained to discover his emotional resources and to learn how to express them as he wishes, depending upon what it is he wishes to communicate. The aim in this chapter then is less to develop character in the old sense, but rather to aid its growth through release, understanding and control, both in oneself and others.

OBSERVATION AND CHARACTER

It will be appreciated that, because improvisation is interpreting and impersonating the situation around us, it is always based upon our looking at people and things around us. Especially is observation important in our work on characterization. People are always full of interest and groups can learn a great deal from visiting places where people congregate and noting their movement and grouping patterns. Large railway stations, supermarkets, fairgrounds, industrial organizations, work sites and markets are some of the useful places for this study.

But then we must also meet the people themselves, talk with them, listen to them and discover more about them. Interest here needs to be genuine and not curiosity only, but there are many

opportunities even in the average day for encountering people at
the bus stop, in the post office, café, car park and so on.

Besides observing people by looking and listening to what they
are saying, we can also learn by noticing the way in which they
express themselves. We need to observe the tone they use and to
see how it is related to occupation, personality and status, and then
notice how this modifies what is being communicated. We should
listen to the pattern of inflexions and find out how much this
conveys apart from the words. Vocabulary can be observed, and
the images used. We can look at the length of phrases and see this
in relation to thought pattern and general personality. Some groups
will find it particularly illuminating to go out with a tape recorder
and interview people in various localities, bringing back their findings for discussion and comment.

Role playing

It may surprise some to realize that most people play several roles
in their every-day life. As they adjust or readjust attitudes to others
they become (often only slightly) a different person. One man in a
single day might play: husband, father, sales representative, colleague, neighbour, local councillor. Each part requires a different
outlook and a different response. A similar adjustment to parts we
are not used to playing will enable us to have insight into what each
entails, help reduce fears and extend sympathy and understanding.

There are many situations which we can explore and in which
we can explore the attitudes and feelings of others. It is also useful
to try out several roles in one situation:

i] An interview for a job. Experience both the parts of inter-
viewee and interviewer for a post in:
a factory
a shop
a bank
a school.
ii] An interview for:
promotion
the sack
a complaint
praise, or a rise in salary.

iii] An interview of someone on probation for:
   theft
   malicious damage
   physical violence
   breaking the probation order.
(Play both the role of the probation officer and that of the person on probation *and* at different points in the period of probation.)

iv] An interview with a parent about:
   school leaving
   drinking or smoking
   a boy or girl friend
   breaking up of the family
   pocket money or clothes.

v] An interview with anyone in authority, such as: a doctor, a headmaster, a policeman, a civil servant, a solicitor, a councillor, a trade union official, an M.P., a parson.
Decide upon the situation with the reasons which have brought about the interview.

With each of these role-playing exercises, it is advisable to decide with some clarity upon the major point of detail governing the situation. Detail of character will no doubt emerge in playing out the situation, and discussion will emphasize some of the major findings. As the work develops there will be greater penetration into aspects of character, and this kind of situation can be returned to, with the emphasis being placed more upon the characters in the situation than upon the situation affecting the character.

Some of the main elements in shaping characterization are:

1. Physical Presence
2. Clothing and Accessories
3. Age
4. Temperament
5. Experience
6. General Attitude and Outlook.

Each of these aspects is clearly interrelated, each affecting the others, and being in turn affected by the others, but for the sake of clarification we will again work on one facet at a time, and then begin to combine them.

I. PHYSICAL PRESENCE

This includes physical build; the way in which a person stands, moves about, and generally deports his physical being, is clearly conditioned by the inner attitude, but in its turn it also helps to shape the mental outlook.

Ask the group to sit in a slouched position and to note how they feel during this. Then ask them to change slowly to sitting upright and let them observe the difference. Next, call for them to walk about with shoulders rounded and hands drawn into chest, and from this to open out to a position in which the head is upright and shoulders and arms are open. Then take the shoulders farther back still to almost military bearing. Build short scenes incorporating these characters and their reactions to each other.

Explore after this three different physical types – the first, who works primarily in a vertical plane and holds himself into the body, rather like a rolled umbrella. Live him through various activities – his daily round, rising, eating, transport, work, meeting other people and so on.

Then take a character who works primarily in a lateral plane, a more square character, physically speaking, and decide what kind of life he is likely to lead. Let him come in contact with characters already met and see what effect they have on each other.

This can be followed by the third more flamboyant character who works in the round, using the space on all sides, with arms, head and body.

When a certain amount has been discovered working on these lines, we can begin to introduce two elements – tall thin character working, for instance, with rounded shoulders and inward-looking personality, or with flamboyant character becoming square and offering opposition in face of certain situations.

Introduce other characteristics and subtleties, using only the physical type as a basis.

Stock characters

There is a tendency in all men and women, either consciously or subconsciously, to wish to group people under headings or categories. We may group people in order to separate them from ourselves, or we may categorize them because we wish to join them. In either case, it makes us feel more secure: in the first case, we claim we are happy that we are not like them; in the second, we are pleased to be assured that we are like them. All this categorizing is a kind of short cut, or shorthand. We select obvious traits of personality and ignore the subtler points. It is a similar principle to making a cartoon, poster or cardboard figure.

In scripted drama this technique has been operating since the classical Greek theatre. The wearing of masks by the actors helped the onlookers to recognize in a moment the kind of person who was being portrayed. Clothing, too, was often a help in underlining particular traits of character and making audiences feel safe with recognizable features and garments. In any society where masks are worn or uniform clothing of any kind is to be seen we find a short cut is in operation for recognition and identification purposes. These masks and standardized garments not only enable onlookers to be able to know the type of person with whom they are dealing, but there is a tendency also for the wearer to adopt the characteristics associated with that mask or uniform. Such stock characters and characteristics may form a useful basis for the portrayal and study of characterization. In their very one-dimensional nature they give something definite and clear to hold on to. They can be a very useful starting-point to the understanding of characterization and, later, groups will be able to develop these into more rounded studies as they introduce other facets of personality and the myriad changes which take place in every character once we begin to penetrate below the surface. For the purpose of satire and comedy generally, where a point of criticism or amusement is being made rapidly, stock character types usefully serve the whole purpose. It is interesting to note, however, that although there exist in every age and civilization characteristics which we recognize as common or stock, every time a stock character is portrayed there is always a large amount of reinterpretation and consequent variation. Every type is modified by the personality presenting him and the situation in which he is portrayed.

Here are some suggestions for stock characters of:

The present-day:

   pop-singer, screaming teen-ager, air hostess, disc-jockey, shop steward, Butlin redcoat, Oxbridge don, Labour councillor, Conservative peer, civil servant, domestic help, district nurse, leather-jacketed boy or girl, two-ulcer executive, American

tourist, Army officer, public-school man, student, tarty bar-
maid.

All these can be enjoyed in comic situations, but we need to
insist on clarity and consistency and truth within the situation.
Then, groups can be encouraged to look at stock characters from
earlier times such as those of:

The Victorian theatre or early cinema:

> destitute girl, handsome young man, distressed mother, drunken
> father, unscrupulous landlord, the Charlie Chaplin type, Laurel
> and Hardy types, contrast between poor and posh, orphan boy
> or girl, workhouse mum and dad, aesthete, doddering judge,
> dashing officer, pickpocket.

The Restoration period:

> fop, old dowager, lecherous husband, debonair young man, silly
> servant girl and man, volatile wife, countryman and woman in
> the town, sycophant.

The Elizabethan period.

> parson, schoolmaster, tradesman, jester, wit, adventurer, Puri-
> tan, opportunist, innkeeper, soldier, justice of the peace, tragic
> king, comic king, romantic hero, tragic queen, tavern layabouts.

The Medieval period:

> bossy wife, precise nun, rough labourer, poor student, stout
> yeoman. In this period also, the stock characters of the morality
> plays suggest single qualities which can form the basis of broad
> characterizations: Youth, Good Deeds, Riot, Avarice and Greed,
> Gluttony, Sloth.

The great period of improvisation in the sixteenth and seven-
teenth centuries was the Italian *commedia dell'arte*. The *commedia*
companies improvised on a given plot outline, using stock characters
who reappeared in similar situations. Present-day television and
radio programmes do much the same kind of thing, but without
improvising, they often lack the spontaneity and variety of the
commedia.

Some of these figures of this early Italian comedy are worth
investigating, and portraying in improvised situations, at the same
time as we are tracing their development.

The commedia *period:*

Pierrot, Columbine, Harlequin, Clown, Pantaloon, Doctor, Captain, Scaramouche, Scapino, Constable and, of course, Punchinello, whom we know better as Punch. (See Allardyce Nicoll: *Harlequin* (Harrap), and *Masks, Mimes and Miracles* (Cooper Square Publishers, Inc., N.Y.)

Anyone who portrays many of these stock characters throughout the ages and thinks at all about them will readily see similar kinds reappearing at different periods. Though the times and often situations are on the surface very different, the nature of man remains with remarkable consistency, and what changes most is our attempt at understanding him.

2. CLOTHING AND ACCESSORIES

What we wear is an extension of our personalities; conversely, the wearing of some garment can help to change our movement and approach. It may help to have a session or so in wearing different jackets and hats and shoes and to have as wide a variety as possible of pieces of material which can be draped in as many ways as we can imagine.

Students might be encouraged to find out how one's personality may be extended or altered by wearing the same piece of material in as many imaginative ways as can be devised – for instance, as a train around the waist, as a cloak, as a loincloth, as a short skirt, a long skirt, as a toga. It is useful to have an assortment of brooches, pins and belts to help in the draping, and these may assist also in the shaping of the character. Students can then be encouraged to develop scenes from the characters they find evolving from these garments, and discussion might follow on the effect the clothes had upon them as well as how far they felt it easy to sustain a role. Similar exploratory sessions might be taken with:

Hats. Cloth cap, military peaked cap, policeman's helmet, fireman's helmet, motor cyclist's crash helmet, oxyacetelyne welder's helmet, wedding veil, and women's hats of various kinds, balaclava, bonnets, trilby, bowler, top hat.

Some amusement can be derived from scenes in which the hats help to dictate the character, but later hats of different kinds become mixed up and actors find themselves trying to sustain the original character while wearing another hat.

Shoes. Hiking boots, slippers, gym shoes, wellingtons, leggings, spats, overshoes, high-heeled shoes, low-heeled shoes, sandals, ballet shoes, moccasins, clogs. Here, people might feel the sensation of wearing the actual footwear and then attempt to develop the imagination to a point at which they can move barefooted, trying to retain the same impression. Characters can evolve from the suggestion of the footwear itself, or a particular character established may go through the changes of several pairs of footwear.

Gloves. Mittens, gauntlets, elbow-length gloves, gloves made of leather, lace, cotton, rubber, asbestos, silk, nylon, wool, gloves worn for protection, adornment, warmth, as part of a uniform, and for burglary.
Again, these will be found to be a useful basis for the development of character and of character in a situation.

Allow time for free exploration of these and for the overcoming of embarrassment, amusement, and general surprise. Then scenes can be shaped, working from the point of view of the clothing. In small groups distribute, say, a large overcoat, a fur wrap, and a walking stick, and ask the people to build a scene, using the garments to help begin their characterizations.

With experience gained in this direction, groups can go on to wear imaginary garments and use imaginary accessories, aiming to make the garment and the characterization as convincing as before. From time to time they can return to the actual clothing and discover if their interpretation was in any way short of the original.

Then they can go on to scenes and situations in which the clothing works against the character and see if, in spite of the costume, they can retain truth of character.

Place characters in costume, in situations which are unfamiliar to the characters being portrayed, and play out these, discussing afterwards the effect of the environment on the person.

Encourage groups to explore modes of dress to which they are not normally accustomed and help them to try out costume which is likely to extend their own discovery of themselves, as distinct from the little part of themselves to which most will want to confine their acting.

3. AGE

Putting years on or taking them off is perhaps the aspect of characterization which is carried out least convincingly in much acting. Most people regard old age as senility and depending upon the point in life from which we view advancing years, anything from thirty onwards can become ancient. The opposite viewpoint also tends to appear: the older we get, the more we regard anyone younger than ourselves as inexperienced juveniles.

In understanding age at all, we need to appreciate that chronological age is not the only thing that counts, and that this is conditioned by the other aspects being considered in this chapter. Many people are either older or younger than their birth certificate. In considering the age of a person as a separate investigation, we can explore some of the physical changes which take place with increasing years, realizing that activity is a thing which keeps the body supple and sprightly, while the more inactive we become the more the bones and muscles become set and respond more slowly.

Groups can experience imaginatively the stiffening and rounding of the shoulders and neck muscles, the tightening of the tendons behind the knee, as well as the sagging of the flesh, the growing abdomen and the necessary readjustment of posture in order to retain balance. Scenes might be worked out involving characters who have reached a greater or lesser degree of lack of physical tone and notice how this, too, affects the mental attitude. We need especially here to guard against overplaying and to stress that the doddering old man may be all right for broad comedy, but is rarely convincing in more serious drama.

Once the physical condition of ageing man has been understood in some measure, we should develop our understanding of age in association with temperament, experience and general outlook, so that a more complete appreciation of our own position in life with that of those younger and older can be developed.

4. TEMPERAMENT

In the early stages of this section of our investigations we can work on people who are, say, predominantly bad-tempered, predominantly light-hearted, predominantly jokers, or predominantly sullen. Take a situation in which all the group can be a character of similar temperament, then someone of opposite temperament.

As confidence and ability is gained in making these temperaments convincing, introduce the physical characteristics already experienced, so that they feel the two working together. Take situations, say, from politics or industry, where these characters might encounter each other, and shape improvisations.

Work next on creating characters whose temperaments are variable – people who find themselves easily affected by a present mood – now cheerful, now sad.

Explore such temperaments as those predominantly patient, and see if truth of the character can be retained, even though the situation conspires against it.

5. EXPERIENCE

Build a character, using variations of the ideas already suggested, and then invent a background for him which seems true to his personality. Let this unfold in a dramatic situation in small groups, for instance, an old man talking to a social worker, a detective questioning a middle-aged woman.

Take another character, building it physically and temperamentally, who this time has lost his memory. Build a scene in a small group in which the character rediscovers his background. Alternatively, let a group verbally build up the background of a person. Then let a student join this group. By questioning he finds out about himself and gradually his personality develops.

A character finds himself in an environment which is not that to which he is used. Invent a scene in which he tries to cover up his background, but some of it is revealed through his actions.

6. GENERAL ATTITUDE AND OUTLOOK

This is the most difficult and subtle of the elements we have considered and is a result of a combination of all the foregoing elements. It really amounts to the philosophy of life of the character, whether he believes he has one or not.

Supposing we take someone who is basically insecure and explore some of the ways in which this might manifest itself in his outlook. It might easily make him assertive, loud, and argumentative. This characterization can be explored by placing him in different situations and even different walks of life. Although he himself would probably not understand the reasons for his insecurity, the actor will need to investigate this and decide whether it is connected with home circumstances, education, job or a combination of all these and others.

Alternatively, we can explore the characterization in which the insecurity is seen more in a shy, retiring attitude which leads to a withdrawal from conversation and an unwillingness to meet people. Similar situations can be developed here and difference in response can be discussed after the improvisations. We can develop circumstances in which these two characters meet each other and explore interpretation of their personalities.

Or take a character whose outlook is no outlook at all, a person without any sense of purpose who is always dreaming of doing things, but never finding the necessary opportunity to carry them into effect. We can put him in different environments in, for instance, a home of plenty, where there is an adequate supply of all the necessities of life and more. Use the improvisation here to discover something of the circumstances which could have led to this state of affairs. Then place him in the opposite situation, where there is very little order and very little material advantage. Test his reaction to various circumstances and see what can be gleaned from these about the causes contributing to his situation.

These approaches can be taken to gain insight and assist our building of characterizations with every variety of outlook from the completely optimistic to the fully pessimistic, from the very secure to the most insecure, and through improvisation we can explore different kinds of optimism and pessimism and different kinds of security and insecurity.

We can take a subjective-objective approach (enter into a character subjectively, then look at him more objectively; for instance, having finished playing him, discuss him with others who shared the experience).

We can investigate aspects of our own personalities and gain some insight into attitudes involved in:

a chip on the shoulder;
an "agin the Government", or any kind of authority;
a distrust of outsiders;

a desire to be with a group;
a desire to be different;
insincerity;
a hardened case;
a confidence trickster;
a perpetual buffoon.

By acting out some of these personalities in a variety of situations, we begin to understand more about the workings of others, and this objectifying of aspects of personality enables us to see more clearly, and come to terms with, these qualities within ourselves.

Ways of building a characterization

It is probably already clear that there are many ways of developing a characterization, and that all can aid the actor in his attempt at a full portrayal. Depending upon the aim and purpose of the improvisation, it may be helpful sometimes to approach the building of characterization in a subjective way.

Throughout this approach to characterization the actor thinks of himself in terms of the character to be portrayed, i.e. when he refers to the person he is impersonating he uses the pronoun "I", and we are concerned with what he is, seen in what he does. Stanislavsky sums up the approach like this, in *Building a Character* (Reinhardt and Evans):

> "From my passing comments throughout you have learned the fundamentals on which our so-called system of acting is based.
>
> "The first of these," Tortsov explained, "is, as you know, the principle of activity, and indicative of the fact that we do not play character images and emotions but *act in the images and passions of a role.*
>
> "The second is the famous saying of Pushkin which points out that the work of an actor is not to create feelings but only to *produce the given circumstances in which true feelings will spontaneously be engendered.*
>
> "The third cornerstone is the organic creativeness of our own nature which we express in the words: *Through conscious technique to the subconscious creation of artistic truth.* One of the main objectives pursued in our approach to acting is this natural

stimulus to the creativeness of organic nature and its sub-consciousness.

"We no not however study the subconscious, but only the paths leading up to it. Remember the things we have discussed in class, which we have been searching for throughout our work together. Our rules have not been founded on any unsteady, uncertain hypotheses concerning the subconscious. On the contrary, in our exercises and rules we constantly based ourselves on the conscious and we tested it out hundreds of times on ourselves and others. We took only incontrovertible laws as the foundation of our knowledge, our practice and our experiments. It was they alone that did us the service of leading us to the unknown world of the subconscious which for moments come alive inside of us.

"Although we knew nothing of the subconscious we still sought contact with and reflex approaches to it.

"Our conscious technique was directed on the one side towards putting our subconscious to work and on the other to learning how not to interfere with it once it was in action."

A contrasting approach takes a more objective view and attempts to stand more outside the character during its creation. Throughout this approach the actor refers to the character to be portrayed as someone outside himself, that is, he uses the third person and says "he". In this approach we find ourselves less concerned with penetration into the subtlety of the working of human personality, but are much more concerned to see the character acting in a given situation and to adopt a critical attitude towards him. The story or plot-line is that which is foremost in our minds, and what the person does rather than what he is in the given social situation. Brecht, in his appendices to "A Short Organum for the Theatre", has a note which reads:

Studying a part means at the same time studying the story; or rather, it ought at first to consist mainly in that. (What happens to the character? How does he take it? What opinions does he come in contact with? etc.) To this end the actor needs to muster his knowledge of men and the world, and he must also ask his questions dialectically.*

* *Brecht on Theatre*, translated by John Willett (Methuen).

And in "A Short Description of a new technique of acting" he tells us:

> there are three aids which may help to alienate the actions and remarks of the characters being portrayed:
> 1. Transposition into the third person.
> 2. Transposition into the past.
> 3. Speaking the stage directions out loud.
> Using the third person and the past tense allows the actor to adopt the right attitude of detachment.*

Then later, in order to clarify some points which had been misunderstood about his approach to acting, he emphasized that he was still concerned with three-dimensional acting. In "A letter to an actor" he writes:

> We shall get empty, superficial, formalistic, mechanical acting if in our technical training we forget for a moment that it is the actor's duty to portray living people.
>
> This brings me to your question whether acting is not turned into something purely technical and more or less inhuman by my insistence that the actor oughtn't to be completely transformed into the character portrayed but should, as it were, stand alongside it criticizing and approving. In my view this is not the case. Such an impression must be due to my way of writing, which takes too much for granted. To hell with my way of writing. Of course the stage of a realistic theatre must be peopled by live, three-dimensional, self-contradictory people, with all their passions, unconsidered utterances and actions. The stage is not a hothouse or a zoological museum full of stuffed animals. The actor has to be able to create such people (and if you could attend our productions you would see them; and they succeed in being people because of our principles, not in spite of them!).
>
> There is however a complete fusion of the actor with his role which leads to his making the character seem so natural, so impossible to conceive any other way, that the audience has simply to accept it as it stands, with the result that a completely sterile atmosphere of "tout comprendre c'est tout pardonner" is engendered, as happened most notably under Naturalism.
>
> We who are concerned to change human as well as ordinary

Brecht on Theatre.

nature must find means of "shedding light on" the human being at that point where he seems capable of being changed by society's intervention. This means a quite new attitude on the part of the actor, for his art has hitherto been based on the assumption that people are what they are, and will remain so whatever it may cost society or themselves: "indestructibly human", "you can't change human nature" and so on. Both emotionally and intellectually he needs to decide his attitude to his scene and his part. The change demanded of the actor is not a cold and mechanical operation: art has nothing cold or mechanical about it, and this change is an artistic one. It cannot take place unless he has real contact with his new audience and a passionate concern for human progress.*

It is important to emphasize that both Stanislavsky and Brecht were continuously practising in the theatre and that their approaches to acting were approaches which evolved and continued to develop throughout their lives. It is too easy for us to overemphasize views of either of these men which we find written at a particular stage in their careers. Beneath the expressed theory, there is a large measure of agreement on fundamental principles. Brecht gives us some of the things which he believes can be learned from Stanislavsky:

The sense of responsibility to society – Stanislavsky showed the actors the social meaning of their craft. Art was not an end in itself to him, but he knew that no end is attained in the theatre except through art.

The star's ensemble playing – Stanislavsky's theatre consisted only of stars, great and small. He proved that individual playing only reaches full effectiveness by means of ensemble playing.

Importance of the broad conception and of details – In the Moscow Art Theatre every play acquired a carefully thought-out shape and a wealth of subtly elaborated detail. The one is useless without the other.

Truthfulness as a duty – Stanislavsky taught that the actor must have exact knowledge of himself and of the men he sets out to portray. Nothing that is not taken from the actor's observation or confirmed by observation, is fit to be observed by the audience.*

* *Brecht on Theatre.*

No doubt Stanislavsky would have found similar points of interest to be learned from Brecht.

The discovery of character is linked with certain questions whether asked in the first or third person, and convincing portrayal may be helped by facing such fundamental issues as: Who am I, or is he? Where am I, or is he? Why am I, or is he, in this situation? When is all this taking place?

When all the analysis has been undertaken and the building process has been carefully developed, the actor needs to feel that he has integrated the person being portrayed and interpreted, so that those who will be sharing in the acted situation can respond on a total level to a unified conception of a personality. Through his artistry the actor is able to bring to himself and others further insight into the understanding of the complex nature of man.

CHAPTER 9

Discovering Group Relationships and Extending Awareness

Besides working as an individual with other individuals, the student needs to learn to respond to the group and within the group. Over and over again in the play, as in life, the person has to be sensitive within the group, and groups have to learn how to respond sensitively to each other. We can begin with work in small groups, so that each of its members learns to sense the presence of the others.

MIRROR IMAGES

In the first instance, call for everyone to be touching one or more members of the group with just the tip of the finger or the edge of the foot. This will help to tune in to a physical awareness. Groups can go on with movement, aiming to respond with some degree of harmony, rising, falling, spreading out, moving around the space at different rates, yet always keeping sensitive to the rest. They can work in pairs in mirror actions, one following the movements of the other, as though in a reflection. This can be developed so that more than two can take part, as though it were a mirror seen in a mirror, and so on, until a fairly large number is involved. They might begin with small occupational movements like shaving, making up, examining the face, and extend this to washing and moving about with the whole body.

Sensitivity would be developed by the actors changing the role, so that the person looking into the mirror becomes the mirror image, and the "mirror image" takes the lead. At first this change-over can be effected at a given signal, or a point agreed on by the individuals. Then, as they become more aware of each other, they will find that they can, in fact, change over roles through a mutual understanding. When some skill has been acquired working in pairs, groups of four can work together so that two now act as the mirror image to the other two. Occupations such as being at the hairdresser's or serving a customer with a hat might start this going, and more complicated scenes involving speech could develop. Then scenes requiring larger groups might be mirrored.

At some points, and for variation, the mirror images could distort the actual action. At first this might be carried out simply for the amusement of all taking part, but then some form of discipline might be introduced, whereby, for instance, the mirror images must decide upon their particular distortion and keep all the distorted movements consistent. A hall of mirrors can be introduced with several people acting and several responding. Sound images similarly may be distorted, aiming first to match sound with vision, and then to contrast the two.

In groups of seven or eight, students can close their eyes and again with touch try to feel the movement response of others, at first moving only with the body, trunk and arms and head, and keeping the feet in the same place. After a time, the groups can cover more space and try the same kind of exercise with hands not touching and eyes open. Another exercise involves students lying on the floor in a circle, facing the ceiling, legs to the centre or the edge of the area, and with little finger touch only. This time vocally they can pass round sound, sensing as the sound approaches them. Then use words, phrases and short pieces of continuous narrative.

UNITY OF RESPONSE

After preliminary exercises of this sort, designed to sharpen awareness, we can begin to work in small groups responding to different imaginary situations. A group can watch the flight of a bird through the air and watch it drop. They can follow a speedboat along the line of the horizon or trace the track of a speeding car at racing trials.

Some of these exercises can be built into a scene and developed with larger numbers.

Groups can then respond to a street accident or some men working down a hole in the road, or a person on the window ledge of the ninth story of a building. Next, the leader can introduce elements of speech and let crowds assemble and disperse as individuals, sensing the group only at the heightened moments of feeling.

THE GROUP AND AN INDIVIDUAL

He can then give practise to enable the individual to become aware of the group in scenes such as those involving an evangelist addressing a crowd from his soap-box, the Lord Mayor meeting complaints from the citizens, the foreman rallying his men, or the occupants of the concentration camp observing the guard. In each of these cases we would work for a different kind of relationship. The group will have its individuals who respond with an awareness of each other and sense the communal feeling against or towards, or about, the one outside the group.

Other variations on this and ways of developing awareness can come from exercises involving a crowd which acts as a group and an individual emerging, e.g. a crowd at a football match where someone faints, or a group of protesters with their leader where another opposing leader sets himself up. We can work also on the fickleness of the crowd who change their mood according to the circumstances presented to them. In these scenes encourage the groups to use cries and calls to demonstrate their unity or disharmony in any particular context.

WORKING WITH TWO GROUPS

When the actors begin to feel some real sense of unity we can introduce groups reacting one against another. It might be as well to explore this group-against-group relationship first in more abstract terms. One group can sit to one side of the space and taking a word or phrase speak this first in unison and later begin to give it some kind of vocal orchestration while the other group move expressively in response.

Supposing we took the word "rumour". The group speaking the word would say it with as much of the quality of the meaning as possible, using the rolled quality of the "r", the long quality of the vowel, and the murmur quality of the last syllable, repeating softly "rumour, rumour, rumour", while the others move amongst each other to this accompaniment, as though they were, in fact, circulating a rumour. In this way both groups have to be aware of each other and after a time they can change functions and experience the action or vocal harmony. Other examples could be a more boisterous kind: Send him off the field! Scandal! Disappointment! Crucify! No more war!

Scenes can then be built involving the two groups meeting in a dramatic situation, for example, a group of police and a group of victims, workers and management, different nationalities.

Conflict is perhaps the most usual meeting of two groups, but we can also explore a more harmonious relationship where the two groups unite their efforts, as with a meeting of two sections of the same army, or the uniting of two religious groups or resolution after conflict between two groups, such as the end of a local feud between two groups of neighbouring countrymen, or a group of young people who are opposing, and have been opposed by, a group of older citizens, sorting out their differences.

TIMING

Another important element in group sensitivity is the matter of timing between individuals and the group, or one group with another. To develop this awareness, we can devise a series of exercises which again involve one group speaking while the other moves. Here the groups together discuss a situation which involves a fair amount of sound and probably some speech, and for this we assume that we are witnessing something like a film running with the sound track played separately. We might take a record shop in which three people are buying a record. The acting group go through the motions of going up to the counter, selecting a record, talking to the assistant, and in turn going into their separate booths, while other groups, doing the sound track, would be responsible for synchronizing the sound of the shop door, footsteps, conversation, booth noises, record-player noises, and even making the sound of the record itself.

This demands a sharpened awareness and a real sense of understanding on both sides. This may need some practice, but, with time, interesting and accurate results can be obtained.

Other ideas include: a factory with workmen trying to make themselves heard; at a hairdresser's salon; in a snack bar; fish-and-chip shop; on the farm; in the kitchen.

Throughout all this group work it may be necessary to remind students of items which they have covered so far in their improvisation. But particularly help to strengthen awareness not only of other people in the group and what they are doing but also where they are in relation to each other and those watching. Insist that the group shape aids the meaning and the communication.

Some work may be needed to remind students of work done on the use of levels, and practice may need to be given so that movement to or from the group and of the groups themselves, one with another, retains its full significance.

CHAPTER 10

Exploration of Mood and Feeling

Perhaps the most neglected aspect of training, whether for the theatre or in education, is that of the emotions. Here is another of those public-school traits of the good Englishman – just as he shows his character best by not having any, so he regards his emotions as things kept well in check, or if possible, to be ignored altogether. In this country we still seem to regard the subject of emotions as one not to be raised in polite society. Certainly the only training of the feelings we acquire is from a narrow experience which teaches us to keep them within strict bounds or ensures that they are suppressed altogether. But this is to ignore the nature of men and women and to stultify an important part of their growth to maturity. We recognize that it is necessary to have a healthy and well-developed physical self, that it is vital to have a fully extended mental self, but so far, we have paid very little direct attention to helping people towards any kind of emotional maturity – a necessity for both sexes if adequate family relationships are to be developed.

Like the body, the emotions which are felt within it need to be kept fit and supple. They, too, need to be exercised, and unless we are prepared to keep using them, we shall be in danger of losing the capacity to feel sensitively. Our emotions and feelings are a vital part of our capacity to build relationships and without having this aspect of our make-up exercised and controlled we are likely to go on making bad relationships or breaking those that might have become more worth while. No one can adequately enter into the understanding and portrayal of a character unless his own feelings are within his command, and in order to bring our emotional states to the point of this awareness we have to be unafraid to recognize and use them. The concept of deliberately exercising feelings like anger and hate disturbs people, yet we have to realize that it is far better to learn to know our emotional selves in the controllable situation like that of an improvisation than to go through life allowing them to shape and misshape us because we dare not recognize them.

We can start with work on an individual level and with feelings which are more everyday and on the surface, and gradually prepare the students for a deeper response and for more wholly involving emotions.

THE INDIVIDUAL MOOD

At the outset we are calling upon them to bring into play some of the imaginative qualities which they have so far been developing. Sitting alone, each one can take, for example, some possession they value rather highly. We can encourage them to see this vividly and to visualize the surroundings where it is normally kept. Then we ask them to imagine that this object has been stolen and to try to feel the disappointment this means. This can be developed so that the experience is shared with another individual who in his turn is asked to respond to the situation. Have several changes of partner, so that the students become used to different reactions and realize that they have to tune in afresh and probably in a different way to every individual.

Urge the group not to force any reaction for the sake of doing something, but rather work on the imaginative reality in order to clarify the inner response. We must also allow adequate time for the development of feeling and so guard against encouraging a slick immediate response. Continue for a while to explore this feeling of sadness, working from things and objects valued, to people about whom we care. Let each one build up first an imaginative picture of someone he or she cares about and imagine that they have arranged some outing or holiday together. Use imagination to make vivid all the preparations and expectations, and then come to the point at which the outing is about to begin. Here introduce the realization that it cannot take place. Again, work with half the group undergoing this experience with others visiting one of the disappointed people and responding to the mood. After this has been slowly experienced with several changes of partner, bring the group together for discussion, so that they can share their introspected feelings. It will probably be discovered that some found it easy, while others perhaps failed to respond very much at all. Some will find that they preferred not to have company while in that mood; others may have appreciated it as helpful. Some probably responded by saying very little; others may have found it necessary to utter platitudes, but whatever the feeling and reaction the discussion will help to clarify the various responses and enable individuals to see their uniqueness as well as what they have in common with others. In any case, the experiencing and then the discussion of the experience in an easy but open atmosphere, reduces the fear many people have of their feelings and enables everyone to realize that it is possible for our emotions to be used by us rather than for us to be in their power.

MOVING ON TO AN OPPOSITE FEELING

In any one session it is as well to keep a balance between contrasting emotions, spending adequate time on each, but overdwelling upon neither. In a session which first explored aspects of sadness or disappointment we could go on to finding out about excitement or a feeling of pleasure. There should, however, be some transitional stage, so that we do not expect groups to jerk from one mood to the next. Before discussion, we might prepare the minds and imaginations by, say, taking the group in imagination on to a hillside or by a river where they can look at the view and breathe in the calm and freshness of the air. From this point we can lead on to the next part of the session.

We can begin our preparation for excitement in a similar way to that in which we felt the sadness. Let the group imagine something they would very much like to possess. Help them to see and make it vivid in the imagination and then they can invent a situation in which the object is achieved either as a present from someone unexpectedly, or by winning a competition. Sharing the experience can then follow, this time, say, in groups of three, each taking it in turn to receive the imagined gift. Give opportunity for varying the groups, so that all have a chance of responding with several different people and then let discussion follow.

With other examples, we can work through a similar progression, but this time trying to put the early preparation, which at first took place solely within the mind, into an enacted situation. In the building of excitement, for instance, instead of sitting alone picturing, say, a tape recorder, students can build a scene in which this desire is expressed, attempting to make the vocalized expression live truthfully with the inner feeling. This is often slow, and patience is needed and at all stages discussion should follow so that the group can say where their difficulties arose and make suggestions as to how these might be overcome.

TALKING IT OUT

Usually with groups who have conscientiously worked through experiences of this kind discussion follows fairly freely, and questions such as, "Did you find it easy to make the feeling true for yourself?" will start a fair amount of discussion, and then one can lead on to asking questions like, "Was it easier when someone else talked to you, or did you prefer them to remain silent? Can you say why one was a help and the other not? Did you find it easier to respond to a feeling of sorrow or to a feeling of excitement?"

Groups will usually suggest ways of helping to make their own acting more vivid and sincere.

LAUGHTER

Kinds of laughter will repay some time in exploration. The group can start with just a snigger, which can be built to laughter, becoming almost beyond control. This kind of laughter can be quite exhausting, so the leader will need to break in in time. Divide the group into threes and ask them to build a situation which would be true for them and which could issue in a more specific kind of laughter, say sinister laughter.

Go on from here to building scenes which involve:

derisive or mocking laughter
sarcastic laughter
sympathetic laughter
risqué laughter
supercilious laughter
polite laughter
hypocritical laughter
embarrassed laughter
full-bellied laughter.

Groups can watch each other and note the different movement patterns which each of these moods create, and can note how much each of these involves the person.

ANGER

The work can then move on to other situations and other moods, as well as to a deepening of the awareness and feeling. If we take the emotion of anger and begin with small group scenes which are designed to produce irritation in one or more of the group, we can then build on to the larger feeling and expression of anger, till it eventually would issue in violence. It is important to let the individuals take matters in the first instance which do, in fact, irritate them. From the outset they are examining the whole nature of anger and will soon discover that it is the tiny and unimportant things that set off those feelings which grow to the compulsive drives which issue into uncontrolled action. With this series of explorations, we could take also the feeling of calm and equanimity and discover the kinds of experiences which lead to this state. Both from discussion and from participation in the improvisations, groups will see that some feelings rise very quickly, while others are established only over a much longer period of time. Gradually they lead on to examples which are less close to their own experience, but through enacting these they will realize what lies within and how, by using the imagination, it can be properly controlled.

RELEASE AND CONTROL

There are feelings of particular strength, such as hate, which some people claim to be incapable of experiencing and yet so close are the opposites of our emotions that we need to unbury each of them in order to have them adequately under control. The tiger from which we run is more terrifying than the one we face. If we lock it in a dark cage, it is only likely to build up its frustration to appear more ferocious at the unexpected moment, unless we make some definite attempt at an understanding of its nature.

Since so many of such moods are rarely allowed any legitimate outlet, it may be that in the early imaginative exercises some loss of control may be apparent. Once the imaginative situation is under way the leader has to be especially observant and sensitive to notice at what point and how he might need to intervene. If a group or an individual becomes too absorbed in a strong emotion, it is important for him either to alter the terms of the situation to bring it more under control or stop it altogether and proceed with discussion. It is especially important on such occasions to conclude the session with a constructive mood if the more violent destructive feelings have been experienced earlier.

Through a similar approach we can learn to comprehend and control such moods as:

boredom —	interest
cattiness —	affection
greed —	generosity
jealousy —	trust
fear —	confidence

and the many variations and manifestations of these vicissitudes of human experience. Some of the deepest experiences are those associated with sorrow and joy over people, and these, too, can be led into imaginative understanding through improvisation. After a time, groups can learn how to sustain personal bereavement following a period of considerable happiness, and to be much more sensitive personalities in the way in which they approach others during a time of particular difficulty. Too often we leave the greatest moments of experience until life throws them upon us, and in this state of complete unpreparedness we seem surprised to see how difficult a readjustment it is. Mature emotions, however, enable us to keep perspective even though we are undergoing a disturbing experience.

RETAINING THE SIGNIFICANCE OF EMOTION

Some people who have not actually experienced such a training feel that there is a danger that emotions become press-button affairs because they are under our control. If we can build an emotion merely by imagining a situation, they feel that this reduces the significance of the "real thing". But does practice in any aspect of living reduce its significance? If we practise a sonata, and even take certain bars out of context to play them over and over again, does this diminish our experience during a performance?

It would seem that, far from being the case that it diminishes the significance, practice makes the moment itself both heightened and under greater control. What must be borne in mind always is that we are not seeking a quicker, more easy response at the emotional level, but a more honestly realized and more truly felt experience. Present-day living conspires to encourage the superficial emotion. Much of the entertainment to which we are subjected only serves to titillate the feelings, and this is the thing which palls because it has such a limited call upon us as people. But, unhappily, constantly being subjected to this level of experience means that we seek some means of evading everything else. How often in the cinema do we notice tears and laughter at the trite and surface situation, yet when there is greater truth in the acting and a deeper penetration into the human situation we find that some people are impelled to find a release through a snigger.

This kind of situation builds up especially at certain phases of development or underdevelopment to a point at which students, finding themselves in a situation calling for emotional response, will let go to a limited level, and if given the opportunity will wallow in this surface emotion. In the early stages this may have some value, especially if discussion follows which leads to consideration of depth of feeling and uncontrolled outward expression. Time and experience, however, should lead on to a more discerning awareness and an extension of the range of feeling. It seems that very often these near-hysterical outbursts are offered as a substitute for genuine feeling, and it is in the individual's recognition of this that value comes.

GROUP MOOD

From this work we lead into the building of group situations in which a mood or atmosphere is created and a contrasting circumstance breaks in, such as a group at a rather hilarious party broken by complaints from the landlord, or a situation making greater demands where a party out for the day on an expedition find themselves stranded in a lonely area. Some of the party become frightened by a stranger, and their fears have to be constructively met by other members of their party.

It is as well to remind those taking part in the group situation that the mood is created by everyone's response. Though they react to a common experience, they are individuals in the crowd. Put them into a street scene, say two or three adjoining tenements where everyone can be busy about his daily routine, and then, at a given signal, ask everyone to rush out into the road where a car has just run over a child. Or they can be small groups or individuals on the beach at a holiday resort when a concert-party arrives and they crowd round in a mood of great festivity. Or all can be out doing their individual shopping in summer in the centre of a large town, when unidentified aircraft machine-gun the streets.

Each of these situations might be developed by sustaining the atmosphere through further plot elaborations or by changing the mood, demanding some contrasting response from individuals. Scenes may be improvised in which one or two people establish a mood which spreads to the larger group; for instance, a fire which breaks out in a large building might be noticed by just a few people and the news travels only gradually to the other occupants.

MUSIC AND MOOD

Aids to the building of mood and atmosphere can be introduced through the use of recorded music – a whole scene can be acted or danced with the music either as a background or an accompaniment, to such subjects as:

> escape
> lull before action
> waiting
> a gay night out.

Or again, sound effects, live or recorded, can be used, either continuously in an improvised scene or at specific intervals to heighten a mood: drums, cymbals, various knocking sounds, bells, as well as such sounds with special emotional content as sirens, hooters, screams.

LIGHTING AND MOOD

Another aid to atmosphere creation is through the use of light and darkness and colour. Groups can experiment in playing scenes in broad, cold light, by warm fireglow effects, candlelight, and, if controlled spotlights are available, single or crossed shafts of light, pools of light against darkness and introduction of coloured lighting on certain areas. Where there is no special lighting available, experiment with existing resources, such as: outside street light or moonlight shining through a window; an open door allowing the corridor lighting to come through into darkened space, and reducing the number of lights in the usual acting space.

In all this, shaping is especially important, and students may need to be reminded to build their improvised scenes with clarity and to keep aware of grouping and movement relationships even though they are occupied with the tension created.

CHAPTER 11

Building a Play from Improvisation

Every improvisation is to some extent a play. Work suggested in earlier sections will have led to the creation of many scenes and some might well have lasted a fair length of time, and by working on them over a period they may have become well shaped and polished. Different approaches will yield different kinds of play. At some stage it will probably be felt desirable to set out to build a definite play from the creative efforts of the group. This means that the play performed will be shaped by those taking part from their particular gifts and talents, as far as these have been developed. Usually the leader will act as the director or co-ordinator, but he will constantly find himself, in discussion with the group, devising new ways of stimulating their imaginations, encouraging them in their response and, with the group, sifting and selecting what to work on further and what to reject. There is a sense in which the play will never be completed, because it will never be static, but the aim will be to devise a fairly satisfactory form within which variations and discoveries can continue.

When a satisfactory shape has been achieved tremendous sensitivity is required by all taking part in order to retain the freshness and vitality without losing the shape and satisfaction in what has been created. One of the hazards of dealing with living things is that the creature grows out of control or to a point at which it no longer fits its clothing. At this point it is as well to recognize the fact, and instead of trying desperately to recapture something which has already been lived through, we need to turn to a new creation. Anyone who saw the film *The Picasso Mystery*, in which the camera watched Picasso painting, will remember how in some creations he went on altering and modifying his work beyond the point of satisfaction, either to viewers or himself. At this point, he shrugged his shoulders and turned to a fresh set of material.

There are all kinds of ways in which ideas may be started:

established stories from literature;
incidents from history;

ideas from newspaper accounts;
word association in a stream-of-consciousness response;
visiting a police court;
characters met in pubs, cafés, trains;
local incidents, such as mine disasters, fires, floods;
listening to music which might suggest stories or characters or
moods;
listening to sounds which could begin a story or set off an
association of ideas.

Then once some ideas have been discussed, the group can consider how the material can be treated.

There must be as many ways of group play building as there are
groups likely to attempt it, and, of course, the method of approach
will be conditioned by the kind of play we decide to build. Alternatively, the kind of play which we find ourselves with at the end will
be the result of the methods we have employed in group creation.

The following main approaches are considered here:

1. Where plot is predominant.
2. Where character is our prime concern.
3. Where dialogue shapes the play.
4. Where a theme is the starting-point.
5. Starting from an incomplete script.

1. WHERE PLOT IS PREDOMINANT

Possibly the easiest way of play creating in the early stages is to take
an established plot which we find in either verse or prose, or in
history, mythology, or literature and explore ways of treatment. It
is necessary to decide whether it is going to be most effective to take
the plot and deal with it chronologically or whether we want to
focus our attention on one aspect and let other elements be revealed.

Straight narrative
For instance, if we took the Norse legend of the Aesir and the
Vanir and decided to bring out the clear struggle between the
forces of creation (the Vanir) and the forces of destruction (the
Aesir) we could look at the legend from its possibilities of inter-
pretation in movement and action.

One day the Vanir sent to the Aesir – on a mission which is not explained – a goddess by the name of Gullveig. This goddess was highly skilled in all the practices of sorcery and by her art had acquired much gold. When, alone, she reached the Aesir they were, it is supposed, tempted by her riches. They seized her and submitted her to savage torture. The Vanir demanded satisfaction. They insisted that either a large sum in money should be paid in reparation, or else that their rank should be recognized as equal to that of the Aesir so that they henceforward would receive an equal right to the sacrifices made by the faithful. After taking counsel the Aesir decided to settle the question by fighting. But in the long and cruel war which followed they were very often defeated by their adversaries. They therefore came to an understanding and resigned themselves to treating the Vanir as their equals. On both sides hostages were exchanged. The Aesir turned over the robust Hoenir and the wise Mimir. The Vanir sent their former enemies the mighty Njord and his son Frey, who, from then on, lived in Asgard and were often confused with the Aesir.*

In the first instance we might discuss in the group the main elements of the story and bring out:

I. A scene in which Gullveig is sent by the Vanir with gold to go to Aesir. The group might invent some reason – to entreat for peace. It might be as well in the first stage to enact the scene without words and later dialogue could be introduced.

II. Gullveig's arrival at the Aesir. They are tempted by her riches, seize her and ill-treat her.

III. They dispatch a messenger to the Vanir with their demand for ransom and equal rights.

IV. A battle follows which could be either symbolically carried out, or with a certain amount of realism, in which first one side and then the other gains the advantage.

V. A withdrawal in which the Aesir allow the Vanir to be regarded as their equals.

VI. Hostages are exchanged, the Vanir sending Njord and Frey to Asgard.

* *Larousse Encyclopedia of Mythology* (Paul Hamlyn).

Such a play could be carried out to a background of appropriate music or sound effects, and dance, song and dialogue might be developed. The first rough run-through would reveal where more imagination was most required and it would be useful to have several groups working on versions of the different parts of the story. Discussion and selection can follow at each phase and some of the better moments might be written down.

In the middle of things

From this kind of improvised development of a play we can turn to a less chronological shaping of the plot. If we decided to take the Oedipus story, we could present it in scenes like this:

I. Laius, warned by the oracle, takes his son, whose feet are bound and pierced, to leave him on the mountainside.

II. A shepherd brings the child he has found to King Polybus, who names him Oedipus.

III. Oedipus as a young man hears of the oracle's prediction and exiles himself from Polybus and his wife, believing them his true parents.

IV. On the road to Boeotia he meets and kills the unknown man, who is, in fact, Laius, his father.

V. Oedipus arrives at Thebes and learns that the Sphinx is devouring all who cannot solve her riddles. He hears also of the promise of Creon that he who delivers the city from the scourge shall marry Jocasta.

VI. Oedipus meets the Sphinx, solves the riddle, and is united with Jocasta.

VII. The scourge of an epidemic over Thebes and the oracle's pronouncement that this is due to Laius's murderer being in the city. Oedipus decides to find him himself.

VIII. The terrible discovery that the man he is looking for is himself.

However, another way of treating the same story might be to begin as Sophocles did with the incidents in scene vii, and let the incidents in numbers I–VI be revealed as reported action during Oedipus's quest, or, as Cocteau did in *The Infernal Machine*, we may begin round about number V and imagine Thebes in a state of unrest, followed by the visit of Oedipus to the Sphinx and so on.

Focus and insight

Or we might take a different approach altogether, making Jocasta the central figure and follow her thoughts and feelings, beginning, say, with her first meeting with Oedipus. Clearly, this kind of approach throws much more emphasis on dialogue and imagination, and in creating plays from improvisation some kind of progression like this will help a natural development from the play of action and incident to the play demanding insight and imagination into human conflict.

Ballads are a useful source of material with children, and folk tales are capable of different kinds of treatment according to the age group. There is a wealth of English narrative verse from Beowulf to Auden.

Almost daily, the newspapers contain paragraphs and reporting which are capable of dramatization. For example, here are two paragraphs from the *Daily Express*:

> A rector, who was asked by a Tyneside chain store if a new employee was honest, told her bosses in confidence that she had been convicted of theft 10 years ago. The woman was told about the rector's note and was sacked.
>
> Said the rector yesterday: 'This is a complete breach of confidence and I intend to do something about it. This person made a slip, but that is no reason why she should be hounded for the rest of her life.'

In the first instance, we can give a copy of this to various small groups and get them to discuss ways in which the story might be treated. Some might place the emphasis on the rector, and some might tell the story placing the woman in the centre of the picture, while a third group might try to keep the balance between the two. It might be treated as a scandal that the woman's theft has been disclosed, or it may be presented as a moral dilemma from the rector's point of view. Scenes might be imagined in which the woman asks for a reference, in which the rector learns of the effect his action has had on the woman. We can imagine that the woman, about whom the paper tells us little, has a family dependent on her, or that she has during the past ten years been a particularly loyal servant to the rector's church.

Such an incident presented like this to groups will call for the exercise of the imaginative powers they have been developing throughout their improvisation work. When many of the possibilities have been explored and groups have looked at each other's versions, we can experiment by combining scenes which seem the most promising and then begin to shape these. Notes can be kept by a group leader and gradually the material sifted until a satisfactory development begins to emerge. Then we need to follow this by work in detail on each of the aspects of the play which we have worked through in previous improvisation sessions. The beginning and ending of the play will probably call for special attention. The characters, the relationships and the mood can be refined until at last we have a play which we would like to rehearse and perform to an audience.

Other starting-points for plays based on plot might be simply the giving of a word or a phrase, such as "independence", "lost", "no luck", "reproach", "tradition", "'tis not so sweet now . . .", "let us grasp this nettle, danger", "the hungry lion roars", "O! brave new world".

We could begin simply by giving the word or phrase to the group and asking them to jot down or say anything which comes into mind as a result of this stimulus. Then some of these can be followed up. Two or more ideas can be combined until a story line is emerging. This can then be developed along the lines of previous examples to the polished play.

As has been seen already, one very useful source of material is to be found in literature and especially dramatic literature. Playwrights have always found it useful to take the plots of other play wrights and give them a new twist or a new setting. Jerome Robbins took *Romeo and Juliet* and placed the conflict in the West Side of New York. For Montagues and Capulets he read Puerto Ricans and white Americans. For Friar Lawrence and his retreat he gave us Doc and his drug store. For Juliet's ball we had a dance in a gym, and so on. Such a story of antagonism and frustration is capable of all kinds of setting – we might think of a dockside story where the conflicts are religious or labour, or the story might be set in the context of political battle, where the parents are on the one hand Conservative and on the other the son is a young Communist. Other plays are capable of similarly being set in a modern situation. Othello's colour insecurity might well be placed in a Southern U.S.A. setting, or we could visualize a middle-class *King Lear* unfolding the present-day problem of age and parent-child relationships. But it is not only the plays of Shakespeare which can be given contemporary settings. Tyrone Guthrie has shown that *The Alchemist* has considerable humour and impact played in modern equivalents, and other Elizabethan and Restoration dramatists, as well as, of course, the Greeks, lend themselves to presentation in terms of the present-day world.

2. WHERE CHARACTER IS THE PRIME CONCERN

In the chapter on characterization we saw ways of approaching character building and in this approach to improvised play making, we begin with the creation of the character. The aim now is to develop the conflict especially within the person and between him and other characters on whom we are working. It would be possible, for instance, to take a study of an historical character and develop this in the light of our understanding of present day psychology.

From history

This is the sort of thing that Osborne did with Luther, and Bolt with Sir Thomas More in *A Man for all Seasons*, and studies are fairly readily available on people like St Francis, who could then be seen not simply as a romantic animal- and bird-lover, but a complex character struggling against his own maladjustments in a medieval world. Groups could be given early incidents in the life of St Francis and asked to discuss them and develop them, bringing out the psychological make-up of the person, then later incidents could be explored in a similar manner, until there was sufficient material to allow for the arrangement and general treatment to be seen.

All kinds of historical personalities will readily spring to mind, such as Plato, Socrates, Nero, Bruno, Boadicea, Augustine, Cromwell, Fox, Wordsworth, Wellington, Pitt, Peel, Mrs Pankhurst, Dick Turpin, Fanny Burney, Samuel Pepys, Samuel Johnson.

Then, as we worked with the creation of a play beginning primarily from plot, so here we decide upon the starting-point and develop the play from that stage, watching the character unfold. This is again more complicated, and at this level it would be necessary to make notes in considerable detail. We could either arrange for each group to have its own scribe or for one writer to be engaged in making notes from the work produced by each of the groups at the different stages of exploration. At some point it will very likely be essential to have one person who is entrusted with the task of final selection and shaping, but if he is sensitive and observant he will all the time be open to the development which the groups reveal. At some point a fairly detailed script may result, but it would always be useful to allow a certain amount of flexibility, so that new insight could be discovered.

From literature

Similarly, literature abounds with characters who could be used as a basis for play building, and it would be especially rewarding if we can apply our understanding to them so that we realize more and more the complexity of the motivation of human action. Personalities like the following would make stimulating studies: Huckleberry Finn, Merlin, Rip Van Winkle, John Gilpin, Pandarus, the Wife of Bath, Moby Dick, Roderick Random, Becky Sharp, Moll Flanders, Pamela, Nicholas Nickleby, Silas Marner, Wordsworth's Michael, Dan McGrew, Frankie and Johnnie, Mr Polly.

Everyday observation would also supply ideas; the obituary column of *The Times* and other newspapers can be read with insight and penetration into the person behind these notices, and especially significant turning-points could be explored through improvisation.

3. WHERE DIALOGUE SHAPES THE PLAY

More than ever today we are discovering the dramatic significance of dialogue, and starting from a conversation overheard in the supermarket, at the bus stop, outside the theatre, or any other place where people meet and talk, we can develop the play based upon the rhythm of interchange and silence.

In the first instance, groups might be given a few lines and asked to develop the language from there. For example:

    i] – He's not a bad player.
        – He's what?
        – He's not a bad player.
        – He played a bad game last week.

– Yes, but he's usually not bad.
– Yes, but he's not good, is he?
– What?
– He's not good, is he?
– No. I didn't say he was. But he's not bad.

ii] Radio is on full volume.

ALICE: Just listen to that.
DORIS: That's the new singer.
ALICE: Isn't it terrible?
DORIS: Just listen to her voice.
ALICE: The way it goes on.
DORIS: It beats me how anybody can listen to it.

Radio blares on.

iii] – He married the girl down the road, the one that lives next
to Mr Black – you know, him that married twice and his
wife came back to dig the garden – his first wife, that is –
'course, she's having a baby – the girl, that is – she's
going into the Salvation Army home – that's the one
where they take the unmarried mothers in – 'course, she's
married, but it doesn't make any difference – they still
take you in.

iv] HIM: I see they're out again.
HER: Do you want one or two?
HIM: You'll never satisfy them.
HER: Fried or boiled?
HIM: Take 'em out and shoot 'em – that's what I'd do.
HER: Well, you can have yours boiled, and I'll have mine
fried.
HIM: They'll be importing them from Germany, if they're
not careful.
HER: I'll have them both ready before the news.
HIM: Then we'll have to get the union in again.
HER: You'd like that, wouldn't you?

It might be useful in such exercises to use a tape recorder and be
prepared to discard a good deal, but from the outset it would be
interesting to observe those pauses and moments of silence which
spring out of genuine appreciation of personality and situation.
Or (as No. iii] above) sometimes the conversation can be built
around a particularly garrulous character – the landlady who talks

incessantly, constantly jumping from subject to subject, sometimes interposing one line of thought in complete opposition to another, or, having introduced a topic, the mention of a name reminds her of all sorts of other irrelevancies. Or a character might repeatedly drop names casually in order to build up his own prowess and make his listener feel more and more out of it.

Once the dialogue begins to flow the place and the situation will most probably present themselves, and although the situation itself may have little development, the conflict will spark off the dialogue development.

In presenting plays of dialogue, groups can experiment with the overlapping of circles of conversation. Begin, say, with two characters apparently talking to each other, but in effect each remaining in his or her own world, such as in the Pinter sketch *The Black and White*. Each of these characters might develop his or her own world and dialogue separately at first, and then come together to interweave their words. Or they may prefer to tune in to each others' wavelengths first, before developing their separate trends of conversation.

From here we can go on to cyclic conversations in pairs, where one couple hold a conversation and another couple have a separate discussion, but the two overlap or interweave and then move on to larger groups. This will call for heightened group awareness and sensitivity as well as a considerable sense of timing. Observation in bars, and coffee-houses, where groups who sit round separate tables holding their own conversations can be heard simultaneously, and the imaginative person will observe the possibilities of developing this on an artistic plane. An example of this in a written play will be found in the first act of Ionesco's *Rhinoceros*.

These ideas can be developed in situations such as the following:

a conversation in a room and another overheard from outside;
one side of a telephone conversation and a conversation in a room;
parents talking, preoccupied, and children playing;
a city or village square, in which we become observers of two or three families at the same time (as in *Sparrers Can't Sing* by Stephen Lewis).

It will soon be seen that we are now becoming very concerned with the rhythm both of individual and community life, and in shaping the play the group editor will be much more concerned with sensing the rise and fall of words and emotions than with more conventional approach to plot and character.

4. WHERE THEME IS THE MAIN CONCERN

Group entertainment can effectively be constructed round a theme. If people are thinking especially of a more conventional play, they will be likely to find their theme and then discuss a plot and character which will highlight or illustrate this.

If, for example, they have decided upon prison reform as their theme, they may look for a specific example from the newspapers, or they may prefer to build a more fictional situation. In either case, they will explore several ways of bringing out their ideas before finally deciding upon a line of approach. Then the shaping and development of the play proceeds very much as already outlined.

There is, however, a place for treatment using the theme as the unifying factor. In this case, we may, in fact, have several smaller plots or situations in which a variety of characters might appear, or the end-product might be a combination of some dialogue scenes, some character scenes, some movement scenes and some songs, all illustrating different aspects of the topic chosen. For example, if a group decided on violence as its topic, we might begin by a general discussion or some research. The group could work in the first instance on looking through newspapers and periodicals of that week for references to violence. They might keep a lookout on television and radio for examples of scenes of violence in fiction or the news and could check their own reading and film-going for other illustrations.

Then comes the time to act out some of these, and almost certainly, even at this stage, different styles will appear. Some might burlesque, some might take a naturalistic approach. Others might present the scene in a different dimension, such as playing it in a music-hall convention, or circus ring, or as a play within a play as in *Oh, What a Lovely War* and *Hang Down Your Head and Die*. At some stage, it would be necessary to decide upon the method to be adopted to shape the piece, and probably out of improvisations an idea would arise. It might simply be a narrator who would link the sequences, or it might be that one aspect of society or life is seen in terms of another – for instance, business seen in terms of a supermarket, politics in terms of a holiday camp, or life seen in terms of any kind of game. In this case each separate item would require to make its own impact and improvisation would be arranged so that the best effect was obtained. Then again, through trying the various sections in different orders, the most effective overall shape might be obtained.

5. STARTING FROM AN INCOMPLETE SCRIPT

Sometimes a group has a member who is keen on writing or perhaps someone outside the group may submit part of a text to the group. By taking this script as a starting-point, the writer can be stimulated into developing his ideas and the group can explore possibilities in and around the script.

We might, first, ask the group to play the script as they found it, each giving their own interpretations of the ideas obtained. Then if, after having read the script through several times and talked about it, they put it by and working from their understanding of it, improvise, many spontaneous developments will result. Depending on how much script is at first presented, the groups can take specific sections of the script and improvise on these.

Should it, say, begin by a small family moving into a new council house, they might take the characters as they know them and play around with the moving in and the various things which might happen. At this stage it would be as well to let them act first and discuss later, and if the author can observe all along, he can draw from the imaginations of each member of the group, and very often some of the things they do will suggest even further possibilities to him. So each sequence can be explored, developed, altered, in the light of these improvisations, and other ideas can be passed back to the groups by the author or leader. Completely new scenes may well emerge which will have been seen to be necessary or effective as a result of this improvised work around the text. At times the group may focus their attention solely on occupational improvisations concerned with the situation; at other times they will explore the characterization. Similarly, mood and climax can be worked on in improvised form, until the author or leader sees the most satisfactory solution. Finally, the author may write his completed script in the light of all this experience. He may decide that at certain moments he wishes to leave the situation flexible, so that improvisation may take place during performance, to ensure that words and situation can build to the most effective climax at the moment of playing.

Several plays have been worked on in this manner by Theatre Workshop (witness *Encore*'s satirical quiz: Name twenty-five people who wrote *The Hostage*), notably Saroyan's *Sam, the Highest Jumper of Them All*. In Ann Jellicoe's *The Knack* we see an instance of the author leaving certain moments open to improvised dialogue.

CHAPTER 12

Observation Posts

At various points throughout the work it might be as well if leaders attempt some kind of stock-taking so that they can find which aspects are in need of special attention and emphasis for future work. Keep in mind the need for encouragement and for criticism to be made constructively, often by members of other groups.

Notice those who still need help with concentration revealed by their constantly looking at the leader or glancing round to see if they are being watched. Are there any who still seem to be left out? Do the students seem to be getting a sense of the development of the session? Are they using ideas or skills practised in the early part adequately in the later work? Is there a discernible improvement in at least one aspect of improvisation? Are the members of the group working quite easily with all students or are some working whenever possible with the same people and so restricting their facility in adapting themselves to different responses? (See Chapter 4: *Beginning and Developing Improvisation.*)

How much confidence have individuals developed? Which are those with least assurance and how can these be helped to gain greater ease in the work? Is this lack of confidence linked with limited absorption? Can the concentration of everyone be improved? How quickly do the groups get on with any assignment given them and how soon can they involve themselves in the work? Does concentration seem to develop throughout the session and is there a point beyond which improvement stops? Does their power of concentration both in time and depth seem to be growing session by session? (See Chapter 5: *Developing Concentration and Absorption.*)

Is imagination being developed on many sides – visually, orally, verbally, kinaesthetically, dramatically? Which of these aspects need most attention? Is discipline in the imaginative work showing some progress? Can students pool imaginative ideas and develop them in a group? Are the students able to work easily and imaginatively together while still fulfilling the aim of a particular piece of work? (See Chapter 6: *Stimulating the Imagination.*)

Is there a clarity and directness in the work and does the dramatic shaping help to clarify even further? Are groups able to develop good communication between themselves? Does this include communicating through listening and stillness as well as talking and acting? Are they beginning to have a fringe awareness of those watching so that the activity is clear to spectators as well? How can the groups be helped to greater firmness in their improvising and shaping? How good are individuals at tuning in to each other on a physical level, effectively using the space, aware of grouping and the visual impact? Can they meet the unexpected easily? (See Chapter 7: *Dramatic Shaping and Communication.*)

Are the groups getting sufficient variety and practice in different approaches to character building? How skilled are they in sustaining characterization both throughout a scene of some length and in meeting contrasting characters? Do some people slip into the same kind of character in most improvisations? In what ways does their portrayal of characters seem to be aiding their understanding of themselves and others? Are they bringing imagination and concentration into their character work? Are they returning sufficiently to direct observation as a basis for characterization? (See Chapter 8: *Building Characterization.*)

Is there enough verbal awareness, so that the same people do not always do all the talking? Is everyone capable of active listening? Which people seem to find this most difficult? Are members of the groups able to help each other out at more difficult points? Are the members of the group aware of each other, and how successful are they in ensuring that each person has an opportunity of undertaking the leadership? How well do they involve everyone in each improvisation? Who are the people who get left out, and why? How can this be overcome? When any individuals break the mood, situation or character in a particular improvisation, what seems to have led to the loss of concentration? Are the other members of the group able to help them re-establish the imaginative response? (See Chapter 9: *Discovering Group Relationships and Extending Awareness.*)

Which of the students seem to be still offering a slick response to emotion? How can those who are still defensive in the matter of feeling be helped in a confident response? Is control in creating mood and feeling evident? What insight into themselves and others have they gained from this work? Is there sufficient sympathy and response to the moods and feelings of others? Are all the students able to communicate a variety of moods and also communicate clearly through the mood? Do some still tend to let the mood overcome them? How rhythmically and poetically can they create atmosphere? (See Chapter 10: *Exploring the Mood and Feeling*.)

PART III

IMPROVISING
using a text

CHAPTER 13

Understanding the Nature of a Dramatic Text

Everyone will, by this stage, be aware that improvisation is concerned with acting where there is no text, or, at its most advanced, where the text is being shaped. For most people, having a text means that there is no room for improvisation and to suggest its use is irreverent and irrelevant – only likely to divert the actor's attention away from his main concern. Much acting in the English-speaking world concerns itself with what it considers to be the two vital questions – What do I say? and Where do I stand? – so that most actors regard words as their first objective, and then everything else, they maintain, can follow.

But we need to face an important question: What is a dramatic text? (See page 126 for a fuller discussion of the difference between a dramatic text and other kinds of text.) A dramatic text begins as ideas in an author's mind which gradually he shapes and reshapes until at last the play in its final form emerges.

Edward Albee in a discussion with John Gielgud* described how he set about the process of writing a play:

"I usually discover that I have started thinking about an idea which I know is going to be a play. This process may take anywhere from six months to two and a half years, and during that period I don't think about the play very much except that I realise from time to time that I *have* been thinking about it, and when the characters who are going to be in the play begin to take shape, I improvise with them.

"I choose a situation that's not going to occur in the play itself and test the characters out to see how they behave in it, how they react within that situation, what they will say to each other in a situation of that sort. And when they start behaving on their own and take over from me and seem quite natural and believable in an improvised situation, then I suppose I know that it's time to start writing the play."

Authors, of course, differ in their approach. Some find themselves unable to do much alteration, some find themselves wanting

* *The Observer*, 18 April 1965.

to do much more. But the process is always the same: feelings and ideas – thoughts – formulation – words. The author may be able to visualize in considerable detail the characters who are speaking the words he writes. He may well be able to hear the inflexion, tone, pace and pauses in the utterance, but he still only uses the recognized written symbols to convey these. He might add, in parentheses, notes to the actor to indicate how he hears the lines spoken, or what kind of movement he sees made at any particular moment, but in the act of committing it to the paper, he writes his play in one dimension only.

In our discussion of acting in Chapter 2 we talked of it as a three-dimensional activity, and one which takes place amongst several other people, also creating in a three-dimensional way, so that somewhere between the writer and his text and the actor and his interpretation of the play we have to find flesh-and-blood response. It happens that, at times, a publisher and/or a stage manager comes between the author and his actor. When a play has been presented in the West End with any degree of success an "acting edition" follows, which often means that the West End production, with its interpretation of setting, movement and vocal expression, becomes incorporated into the text, so that, just as with texts from an earlier age, we are never quite sure which is the author's and what has crept in since he put down his pen. With Shakespeare the situation is perhaps most confused. In fact, we have no manuscript extant, and of the printed versions available the variations are considerable. Most producers seem to trust the particular editor of the text they are using, accepting his punctuation, verbal emendations and scene and act divisions, even in notable cases like *Hamlet* accepting his sequence of scenes. The Peter Hall–John Barton partnership is a notable exception in that they clearly not only compare variant readings, but produce their own version, helping the author out with the odd line or two or three hundred!

Another person who may come between the author and the actor is the translator. Many of the major figures in world drama come to us only through translation, so that we are very much in the hand of this middleman in our attempt to understand the original author. The most complicated and difficult kind of translation is that of verse drama, where direct equivalents are not available and, in fact, any kind of imagery, idiom or rhythmic pattern can lead us into special problems. We can see something of this problem in comparing the following versions of the last few lines of Ibsen's play *The Wild Duck*:

Translation by Mrs F. E. Archer:

> RELLING: Oh, life would be quite tolerable, after all, if only we could be rid of the confounded duns that keep on pestering us, in our poverty, with the claim of the ideal.
>
> GREGERS (*looking straight before him*): In that case, I'm glad that my destiny is what it is.
>
> RELLING: Excuse me – what *is* your destiny?
>
> GREGERS (*going*): To be the thirteenth at table.
>
> RELLING: The devil it is.

Translation by Una Ellis-Fermor:

> RELLING: Oh, life would be tolerable enough, even so, if we could only be rid of these infernal duns who come to us poor people's doors with their claim of the ideal.
>
> GREGERS (*looking in front of him*): In that case, I am glad my destiny is what it is.
>
> RELLING: May I ask – what *is* your destiny?
>
> GREGERS (*on the point of going*): To be thirteenth at table.
>
> RELLING: I wonder . . .

Translation by Michael Meyer:

> RELLING: Oh, my life would be all right if we didn't have to put up with these damned creditors who keep pestering us with the demands of their ideals.
>
> GREGERS (*stares ahead of him*): In that case, I am glad that my destiny is what it is.
>
> RELLING: And what, if I may ask, is your destiny?
>
> GREGERS (*as he goes towards the door*): To be the thirteenth at table.

In any case, the author would rarely regard himself as being the best person to interpret his play fully. Of course, he knows what it is about, and knows what he wants to say, but in many cases his feeling for the shape, relationships and dialogue was intuitive and not intellectualized at the time of writing. Anyone standing as close to a work of art as an author must of necessity obtain a foreshortened view. The process of writing is a drawn-out one, the process of playing a much speedier affair. While in the process of writing the author may find elements of his work changing, and it is difficult for him, even if he is keen on revision, to step back from it to a sufficient distance to grasp the play in anything like its full perspective.

Similarly, when the actor comes to the text he needs to approach it with some understanding of what it is he is going to work on. He is given a centre or focus and he has to build on and around this in order to arrive at the living moment which he will share with the audience.

The actor is not a mechanical man with a recorded programme which goes on throughout the play. He is the one artist who is called upon to use himself as a full human being at the moment that he executes his art and shares it with a public.

The text, then, is not something which he has to commit to memory, like a shopping list, or a mathematical table: it is something of which he has to come to a full understanding, in order to be able to re-enact those moments in time with his fellow actors. Instead of the all too frequent process of words – moves – character – thoughts – feelings – live acting, he needs to reverse the sequence and work from his feelings – thoughts – character – moves, and finally arrive at the words the author wrote because he has a full understanding and realizes that no other words or word order will quite serve the same purpose. This, it will be seen, follows a similar sequence to that which the author underwent. The very fact of having to commit a play to paper means that the author is offering us at best a dehydrated meal. The actor's process must include an understanding of this, in order for him to realize what his creativity must give.

All too little is known, at this stage of things, about the nature of man's memory. But sufficient experience can be called upon to establish that, where understanding is involved, memory becomes easier. On the stage, with his fellow actors, the actor rarely gets worried about remembering what he calls his "moves". These are physical things and are appreciated with the body. He does, however, often worry about remembering his part, and his anxiety is greatest when he regards this as his "lines". The anxiety remains because he has kept the words on the plane of the intellect and relied almost entirely upon pure memory. In life, when we are holding a conversation, we do not have "a dry". It is true that at times we say, "Where was I?" or "I forgot what I was saying", or "I've lost my train of thought". This is due to loss of concentration rather than loss of memory, and usually all we need is the briefest reminder of the trend of conversation for us to be back in the flow of conversation again.

In the acted situation, if understanding at a deep level has taken place, and the concentration goes for a moment, usually all that is necessary is for us to see who we are and where we are, and with whom we are, for the situation to become abundantly clear. The exact words may have gone, but the approximate language and the mood and situation, as well as the direction, will remain. However, should the loss of concentration be so great that we fail to be put back on the line by this realization, one of the other members of the team will easily be able to bring us back into the concentration of the moment, by responding in mood and character. If acting remains a group concern, very little need be broken for the actors and nothing need be perceptible to the audience. The business of a lapse of concentration on the stage is linked with the whole emotional state of the actor. His return to the full state of concentration on the situation will be directly related to the speed at which he can rid himself of any emotional blockage, and this is where a good team approach to the acting situation will be of additional benefit.

The prime need is that the learning process should have been one of understanding with the whole person – physical being, mental being and imaginative being. If you want to learn to swim, you may well read a book about it, and then jump in the water and practise it. You might well learn off the instruction manual by heart, but ten to one your swimming will not be very good. Most people recognize that it would be more sensible to read the instruction manual through, and then take it, section by section, exploring each part first on the land, and then in the water, finally putting it together in the full swimming action. If you work this way, you will probably return to the book over and over again between moments of practice, in order to check that you are on the right lines, or in order to find out answers to questions that the practice has shown are needed to complete your understanding.

Swimming is a physical activity, and requires understanding in mind and body. Acting is an even more wholly involving activity, and requires therefore this understanding on a full level. We are often told about someone else's experience and we think we know what they are talking about, then one day it happens to us, and we discover that our understanding has reached a new dimension. In the rehearsal of the play it is not sufficient to understand with the intellect and then go through the physical motions. Rehearsals are there to afford an opportunity for us to capture the experience which the words can only symbolize. We need to get at what Stanislavsky came to refer to as the "under-text", but which we might think of as the over-and-around-text, which gives the three-dimensional quality to playing. It will be seen that, with this kind of comprehension of a text, there is no place for a prompter, and still less for the actor on stage who will whisper the forgotten line to his unfortunate colleague. In any case, one does not forget what is experienced in rehearsal and kept alive by continued practice, and this is the contribution of improvisation.

The aim of improvisation in the rehearsal of a play is to explore the text on various levels. The work may well be done without the text in the hand, and (especially in the early stages) with no conscious attempt at *remembering the lines*. What is taking place is the much more important process of *understanding the feelings, thoughts and words*. Improvisation tries to encourage the actor and director to take an overall grasp of the play at first, then to explore it in its parts, and finally to synthesize. In the early stages there might well be a deliberate attempt to prevent the actor from coming too close to his lines until he has grasped an understanding of the play overall.

At first, for the company experienced in quick learning of lines and inexperienced at improvising and approaching the text from understanding, it will obviously be a longer and more difficult task, but, with practice, much improvisation in rehearsals leads to a quicker rehearsal process. Above all, acting based on this fuller understanding must have a much greater depth and richness. The same is, of course, true if we are working on the play for primarily educational reasons. If we experience the text, we are coming more in harmony with the author's intention and adding fuller awareness to our understanding and enjoyment.

A note on the difference between a dramatic text and other kinds of text

A dramatic text is unlike any other text. When an author writes a novel he commits his ideas to the page and expects them to remain there only to be read in private. The work which he has written is complete in itself, as something committed to paper. It was in the first instance an imaginative conception of characters and situation, and in choosing the novel as his form he selected this out-of-time means of recording his feeling. His intention is that any visual or aural impact shall be made on the reader purely through his imagination. The work of the poet is not dissimilar. He is concerned more particularly with the rhythmic pattern of his words, recognizing that these add a further dimension. He is careful for the sound equivalents of his language, and though he may well hope that his readers may speak his work aloud, he is not concerned with the visual impact other than through the imagination. But the playwright is conceiving his work in terms of its actual visual and aural and emotional stimulus, as well as that achieved through the realm of the imagination. He is limited at this point in history to the form of recording which we find most convenient, namely the written word on the page. He is one man thinking of the interplay of many men, and this interplay he envisages taking place at definite moments in time.

The writer of a novel or a poem regards his statement as complete on the page. He may well hope that this statement will spark off many responses within the reader, but he does expect himself to be the sole means of this communication. The man who writes a play knows that his statement on the page is his attempt only to convey to the actor what he wishes him to represent to the audience. Through variety of living interpretation will come the full impact of the piece. He does not attempt even to give a full description of all the subtleties of movement, tone, inflexion, pause and pace which will interact in order to build the atmosphere and feeling that will exist only at a given moment in time and make the communication. In a novel about the way in which the inmates of the asylum of Charenton performed the persecution and assassination of Marat under the direction of the Marquis de Sade, we would gain understanding of the situation and no doubt feel something of the impact of a play under such conditions. But if we actually sit at a performance of the play by Peter Weiss which interprets the same material, we know with our whole being in a way in which no novel or poem could possibly affect us.

It seems, therefore, strange that we should have come so far in educational progress without recognizing this difference sufficiently to make us want to approach a dramatic text in a different way from the text of a poem or novel. Universities (even drama departments), colleges and many schools still seem to persist in the one-dimensional appreciation.

CHAPTER 14

Seeing the Play as a Living Whole

A play is a unity. It may be divided into acts and scenes, episodes or phases, but it is meant to be seen and experienced at a more or less continuous session in time. It is not a series of lines of dialogue spoken by different people. The thoughts and expressions of the characters are interrelated. Even when they seem to have a certain amount of *non sequitur*, such an arrangement is carried out in order to make a point or create an effect. It is so easy when one is studying a play to concern oneself with the parts rather than with the whole and so miss a great deal of the point. We need also to recognize that the wholeness of the text exists in its physical realization and its three-dimensional nature.

The problem is, how can one act a play before it has been studied fully? It is sometimes possible to go and see the play in performance which enables us to grasp something of its unity, provided always that this has been appreciated and fully understood by all the members of the company. In fact, this may be difficult to achieve. There are some actors still who maintain that if they are not present in the acting of a scene they should have little or no knowledge of that scene, believing that somehow this will enable them to play the scenes in which they do appear with greater reality and truth. But here we need to recall our earlier discussion about the actor's concentration and awareness. True, the character he is interpreting is not present in some of the scenes and this is where he needs to use his imagination. As an actor who is a member of a team, it is essential that he is fully aware of all aspects of the play in order that his part may be played in the right relationship to the rest. When he comes actually to perform the play before an audience is the time for him to focus his concentration upon the character played and hold it on the immediate relationships the character has with others. The rest of the play will then be part of his fringe awareness.

We are still then faced with this difficulty, of feeling something of the living whole of the play before we have grasped it completely. Again, group work is necessary, and the first process must be to read the play through either individually or as a group in order to gather as much of the gist of it as we can. The second reading is likely to be broken by discussion, in order to grasp the main elements of the structure. Here, it is as well for someone to keep notes of the points agreed upon. These are really milestones or signposts throughout the play and serve as guides when we improvise. At this point less attention is being paid to detail than to the overall picture. It is often as well at this stage to force the pace a little, so that the student or actor has to go for the essentials. Of course, this means that he has to decide what is essential. Then, once the whole text has been worked through in this manner, groups begin to rehearse an improvised version of the play based on their notes or "signposts". It may be easier, if the play is long, especially difficult, or the group inexperienced, to divide up the play, giving each group one section only to work on. If desired in the early stages, these signposts or brief reminders may be placed about the acting area so that actors have something to guide them and so ensure that the play keeps moving forward in the desired direction. During the time of rehearsal groups should be encouraged to leave the texts to one side and to improvise as far as they can, moving and acting and being and helping each other forward to the best of their ability. Over and over again they will find they are going outside the text, or getting lost within the text, or unable to carry on, and these are the moments when they will return to consult the text. The important thing now is that they go back to the text in order to "use" it. They come to it with questions in their minds, such as, "What follows from here?" "How do we get from A to B?" "Why does she use this way of expressing herself?"

It is surprising how quickly one becomes acquainted with the text in this way. The same time spent simply reading the text achieves nothing like so much familiarity or understanding. No conscious effort is made to remember "the lines", but in grasping the thoughts and the sequence it quickly follows that the words themselves are retained. The living text now becomes the important thing for survival, instead of the mechanical words. Energy and effort is now directed towards understanding rather than towards remembering, and experience has shown that it is the understood things which are easiest to recall. When one is *trying* to remember, effort is used in trying, and tension is built up. This is clearly seen in the way in which some actors and actresses stamp or click their fingers when they are trying to remember. This indicates the mechanical aspect of their memory work, whereas if we were recalling a thought finger-clicking would be the last thing we should do. After some experience of improvisation, students and actors prefer to be asked a question about their characters or the situation in which they find themselves, in order to regain the continuity, rather than be *told* anything, or be given a "prompt". It is interesting to notice that when a person in the theatre requires a "prompt" it is often at a most unusual moment, and sometimes even in the middle of an obvious thought sequence, so that if the understanding were going along with the utterance this "dry-up" could never happen. Sometimes, indeed, a "prompt" has to be given at the same point in the text over and over again. Instead of a question being raised in the actor's mind at this point and his returning to the text to find some reason for progressing from point f to point g, he simply accepts being told the next few words, so there is little hope of his retaining anything while he is relying on "pure" memory and building up the tension, instead of releasing it around that place of difficulty.

When the rehearsals have given a certain amount of confidence in the progression of the play, it is time to share the improvised version with the others. Usually, groups will feel hopelessly insecure (which is perfectly natural, because we are only at the beginning), but often they will surprise even themselves at how much they have grasped when it comes to the moment of presentation. With very little experience, it is possible for groups to present plays which would, if played fully, run for under two hours in an improvised form lasting about an hour and retaining to a remarkable degree essential elements of the text. It sometimes happens that in these improvised presentations we discover misinterpretations of the text, uncertainties and insecurities which at this early stage it is easy to refer back to the text. On the other hand, it also happens that some of these misunderstandings or inadequate realizations (on the mental level) are grasped in the very act of playing them out. At this point in the discovery of the life of the text the prime concern is to feel something of the overall shape and continuity of the piece and to grasp something of the interrelationship of the characters. When it is contemplated that the play is to be performed as a finished production, it is advisable to complete this section of the work before casting takes place, or if casting is already completed to ensure that at this point actors are not inter-preting the roles which later they will be studying in greater detail.

With some plays where the plot line is particularly strong it is fairly easy to agree upon the main sections of the play and to establish the signposts. If we took *The Long and the Short and the Tall*,* we could recognize quite quickly that the play moves for-ward in twelve sections, each building to, or built upon, a moment of tension. It would probably be necessary, therefore, only to grasp these for a fairly accurate improvisation to build. In the longish sequence towards the beginning of Act 1, where Bamforth holds the centre of the action, after Johnstone and Mitchem have gone out, it may be necessary to work in slightly greater detail, the impro-visers making notes to remind themselves of the main development of this part of the play. It might go something like this:

I.   Bamforth/Evans – Welsh prowess – barmaids – chapel.
II.   Bamforth/McLeish – pack it in – chasing stripe – insist on backing up N.C.O.s.
III. Bamforth turns to Whitaker – song-and-dance routine – Whitaker – something on set. Bamforth mocks this. After further try on radio, Whitaker abandons it.
IV.   Bamforth/Evans mock week-end pass routine.
V.   Whitaker tries set again.
VI.   Bamforth reads from *Ladies' Companion and Home*.
VII. Evans narrates part of the serial.
VIII. Bamforth reads letter to Margaret Denning.
IX.   Bamforth/Smith talk about Smith's home and family.
X.   Bamforth rags Evans that his wife will have had two youngsters while he was away. Fight follows.
XI.   Whitaker, still on set, hears voices.
XII. Bamforth rags Whitaker and moans about the rations.
XIII. Bamforth narrates his imaginary escape if the Japs come, and rags McLeish.
XIV. McLeish is roused to anger and the two rile each other and start a fight, as Johnstone and Mitchem return.

It is nearly always true that it is necessary to jot down slightly more notes where the play or the section of the play hinges on

* *New English Dramatists* (Penguin Books: PL 49).

dialogue or back-chat, but once the groups have played such a scene once or twice with their notes, and have gone back to the text to sort out difficulties, the sequence will be grasped and they will soon find that they can dispense with most of these. One of the interesting things about this part of the work is that, if done well, it proves of extraordinary value when the groups come to consider the shape of the play in greater detail.

Modern plays built on very short speeches and especially terse dialogue sometimes seem to present the most difficulty. In the stage of early reading these plays sometimes appear almost shapeless, but after a brief amount of reading and discussion it is possible to grasp points for reference, and out of these the pattern of the play very often becomes evident. Here is how Harold Pinter's play *The Dumb Waiter** might be signposted in the very early stages of improvisation, designed to help the group to see the play as a living whole:

I.   Ben at newspaper – man of eighty-seven – lorry.
II. Gus to lavatory – returns – tea.
III. Ben at paper – child of eight – cat. When is he getting in touch? – Gus.
IV. Gus questions re delayed action of lavatory flush – condition of the place.
V.   Gus complains about the place and the conditions of the job.
VI. Gus questions Ben re his stopping the car on the way here – bad streets.
VII. Birmingham – Villa – disputed penalty. When is he getting in touch? – Gus.
VIII. Like to see Spurs play.
IX. Envelope appears under door – matches.
X.   Light the kettle/gas argument – builds to Ben at Gus's throat.
XI. Gus exits – returns.
XII. Gus asks who is it going to be? Ben checks gun.
XIII. The gas has gone out – neither have any money for meter.
XIV. Discuss whose place it is and all the other places – conditions.

* *New English Dramatists* (Penguin Books: PL 49 and Methuen).

XV.	Gus recalls the last one – a girl, and the mess.
XVI.	The dumb waiter with first message – steak and chips, sago pud – tea.
XVII.	Funny – place once a café – who's got it now?
XVIII.	Second message – soup – liver – tart – must send something up – their bag examined.
XIX.	Biscuits – choc – milk – Eccles cake – tea – crisps – waiter goes up empty.
XX.	Gus still wondering about the place – gas ring/ownership.
XXI.	Third message – Greek dishes.
XXII.	They itemize their goods into the waiter and send them up.
XXIII.	They check their guns – Gus still wondering – the place – Wilson.
XXIV.	Fourth message – Chinese food – tea returned.
XXV.	Ben about to write note sees speaking-tube – Gus uses it then.
XXVI.	Ben hears complaints of the goods.
XXVII.	Gus regrets sending anything – imagines the plenty above.
XXVIII.	Ben gives instructions to Gus, who repeats them.
XXIX.	Missed something out – Gus hasn't taken out gun.
XXX.	Gus to lavatory again.
XXXI.	Gus returns and questions – matches – upstairs – moved out – in – no sense in it – why are they being put through it?
XXXII.	Fifth message – scampi. Gus worked up – nothing left – Ben hits him.
XXXIII.	Ben returns to the bed and the newspapers – reads and comments – Gus echoes him.
XXXIV.	Gus goes out.
XXXV.	Ben answers speaking-tube – learns he has arrived and will be coming in.
XXXVI.	Ben levels revolver at outside door – Gus stumbles in.

After a few rehearsals the players working on this piece will probably find that they are beginning to grasp the flow, and will be able to reduce their guide lines to something like this:

I.   Ben and newspaper – incidents – Gus lavatory.

II.   Gus worries – the flush – the place – the job – the stopping of the car – news from the boss.

III.   The envelope – matches – gas – no money.

IV.   Gus worries – whose place – the girl – clearing up.

V.   The dumb waiter (1).

VI.   The dumb waiter (2) – goods to be sent up.

VII.   The dumb waiter (3) – Greek – goods sent up – guns
checked.

VIII.   The dumb waiter (4) – Chinese – speaking-tube – complaints against food.

IX.   Ben gives Gus his instructions.

X.   Gus still worrying.

XI.   The dumb waiter (5) – Gus agitated.

XII.   Gus exits – Ben speaking-tube – Ben faces Gus.

This latter is the kind of breakdown which it is possible to have
around the acting area, and it can be referred to without breaking
the mood or sequence. In a play like this, where actual notes are
props, the actors can have these clearly marked and can read the
menus from them at the appropriate time. At all points actors need
to be encouraged to rely upon themselves rather than the notes, and
after they have worked on a few plays in this manner they will find
that the mind is capable of retaining quite an elaborate sequence,
especially when it has been gone over in action a time or two.
Indeed, some actors never need to rely upon such an outline when
they come to present their improvisation to the rest of the group,
and even at this early stage show remarkable grasp of actual
dialogue as well as of the overall unity of the text.

Clearly, this can take a very long or a very short time, but as all
we are aiming at here is an introduction to an appreciation of the
play as a living unity, we wish to spend only as much time as is
absolutely necessary. If we assume that the people who are going
to undertake the improvisation have already read through the play
on their own, then they might spend one session talking about the
play and agreeing upon the signposts. Another session would be
spent on improvising using these signposts and referring back to
the text. Most groups would then find they were able to improvise
the play, using only the minimum of notes on the acting area or
requiring no external aids at all. This work is purely introductory,

but it will be seen that anyone who has worked on a play in this way has a good foundation for the more detailed work which follows.

For some purposes this might be as far as it is necessary to develop one's understanding of a play at a particular time. For instance, supposing a play is being studied in considerable detail, but actors wish to get to know other plays by the same author, or look into plays of the same period, these other plays could be studied at this level only. Normal reading leaves understanding of the play in the single dimension, but an improvisation on these lines, besides establishing the play more firmly in the mind, affords opportunity for first-hand discovery of the piece as dramatic relationships in a situation existing in time.

It is possible for some actors to have rehearsed a play over two or three weeks, to have played in it for a further period of time, and at the end to know less about the play than someone who had worked in this way for the three suggested sessions. In schools the situation is often far worse. Most fifth- and sixth-formers approach a text on analytical appreciation for at least a year, and at the end have no clear overall understanding of the play and especially of the play as a living whole.

CHAPTER 15

Understanding the Kind of Play

Before trying to discover the meaning and purpose of particular sections, lines or words in their contexts, we need to have grasped something of the overall mood of the play. Very often the preliminary work done in improvising to arrive at some understanding of the unity of the piece will have given us a clue to its tone, especially if the actors have grown sensitive to working with each other and can imaginatively respond to the author's script.

Discussion will undoubtedly follow the early work, and it may well be that those who have been watching and those who have been playing may have felt differently about the approach. It is on this discussion that further improvisation can follow, designed to lead towards fuller understanding of the kind of drama on which they are working.

> The best actors in the world, either for tragedy, comedy, history, pastoral, pastoral-comical, historical-pastoral, tragical-historical, tragical-comical-historical-pastoral, scene individual, or poem unlimited.

It would not be difficult to add to Polonius's list other possible classifications, for in every decade at least one new kind seems to enter the table. But the aim here is not to give a play a neat label, for that will only tend to lead to more difficulties than it solves. Suppose it has been decided to work on Marlowe's play *Doctor Faustus*. It is not a great deal of help to call it a tragedy and think we have finished. Marlowe himself titles it, "The tragical history of Doctor Faustus", but the task of how to present the play is still not much easier. Really, we can only discover the kind of play we are working on by feeling its tone in practice. Everyone in the group might take the scene of Doctor Faustus in his study at the beginning of the play. Once Marlowe's action and something of the treatment has been grasped from reading it aloud and moving it, the actors can put the text to one side and begin on improvisation. Follow this with the visit of the Good and Bad Angels and aim to discover what lies behind their visit. In this improvised work the

Good and Bad Angels might play their part in this scene in different ways and moods to test the effect both on Faustus and the overall tone of the scene. They might see themselves as medieval personifications or as less materialized embodiments of Faustus's inner conflict. They can play the scene in seriousness and try it in a more comic light-hearted vein. Discussion with other groups can follow as to what the author seems to be aiming at. Try the same approach with Faustus and the Devil in order to determine the function of Mephistophilis. After this the whole scene might be played through leading up to the entry of Wagner and the Clown. In these improvised explorations it soon becomes clear that there is, in fact, a change of approach, a change even of mood and intention, by the time Wagner and the Clown are alone. But played out in several styles, groups soon discover that here is a deliberate piece of comedy which, seen in its context, makes its own comment and highlights the gravity of the scene which precedes it. All through the play changes of texture can be felt in the improvisations. The introduction of the Seven Deadly Sins in its context explored from several manners of playing can help this interlude to gain a more integrated place in the action. And so, working on through the play, everyone becomes aware of the alternation and changes in mood and impact, and can see that if the play is to be taken as a unity these need to be understood. In this way everybody comes to a realization of the styles within the overall pattern and ceases to be embarrassed by them.

Even with plays where the change of textures is less obvious, it is helpful if the actors can sense the kind of playing demanded. It is not possible to approach *Romeo and Juliet* in the same frame of mind as, say, *King Lear*. Early improvised work which allows the actors to feel the atmosphere of Verona and the conflicts which bring out the tragedy of *Romeo and Juliet* give an opportunity for the players to tune in to the size and quality of response demanded. Similarly, it is much more helpful to all the actors about to work on parts in a play like *King Lear* if they can, in improvised form, work through the whole play at this early stage, concentrating their attention on the magnitude of the piece. This experience can save a great deal of talk and explanation, because it is a quality linked with physical awareness and response more than the intellect. A good many of the usual anxieties and difficulties over much Greek tragedy could be avoided if actors were able early on to feel what it is like to interpret these plays out of doors in a large space, and very often we can come nearer to understanding an author's aim and approach if we can physically respond to his text in something akin to the conditions for which he was writing.

Writers of plays called "comedies" present an even wider range of approaches than those of tragedy. For some playwrights their aim was conscious and specific. Ben Jonson, for instance, knew exactly what he wanted and usually made his intention clear. It is only necessary to read and improvise a play like *Volpone* to see the crispness of his dramatic method. In this play, if we improvise the first scene in which Volpone, simulating near-death, meets his "clients", it is possible to sense the spirit of the fox and the clarity of portrayal of his "birds of prey". This, followed by improvisations of the later visits of Celia and Lady Politick Would-Be, again helps the actors to comprehend the directness of Jonson's purpose. Improvisation taken on to Volpone's appearance at the court and his final mortification makes clear the sharpening of the moral tone with the gradual damping down on humour. It is important for all actors, even at an early stage, to feel the way in which Jonson moves from the near-farce of the opening to the near-tragedy of the end in showing us the self-destructive nature of man's avarice.

The various textures of comedy throughout the plays of Shakespeare are full of opportunities for exploration through improvisation. Furthermore, this approach has the advantage of enabling even comparatively inexperienced players to work on discovering the plays through acting without too much anxiety in coping with the language in early rehearsals. A play like *The Merry Wives of Windsor* might well seem unpromising to a group at a static reading, but once they put down the copies (keeping them within reach for reference) and begin to enact the scenes, the boisterous farce emerges. They become aware of Falstaff's amorous advances to Mistresses Ford and Page, watch Master Ford's disguise, see the irony of Falstaff's plotting his own discomfort, laugh at him in the laundry basket, help him dress up as the old woman of Brentford. The play, with its comedy of character and situations, springs to life. They discover its farce, feel its pace and recognize its calls of broad playing and crisp effect.

In a comedy like *A Midsummer Night's Dream* it is necessary to sense the difference in playing demanded by Puck and the fairies, Bottom and the mechanicals, and the lovers. When an actress is called upon to play Helena, for instance, without having considered the play as a whole and its changes of mood which build together to form a unity, it is too easy for her to play it in the wrong style. If we take some of the scenes in the wood for improvisation, we can let the lovers play out some of the sequences in an endeavour to give them insight into the situation. Helena can play through some of her mental and physical preparations in following Lysander and Hermia and of the various frustrations which follow, leading to the complete reversal of her fortune, when, instead of being loved by neither Demetrius nor Lysander, she finds herself being adored by both. At the end of a whole series of explorations into Helena's frame of mind we can face the group with the questions: Is this predicament funny, and if so, why? This should lead to a consideration of what humour is inherent in the scene, its situations and relationships, and what humour arises from character, and the way in which the character is played. Then everyone can go through the experience of playing out some of the scenes in which the mechanicals consider and rehearse their play, and again discussion can follow to discover where the humour lies. In each case the fun is physical, arising out of a physical situation, and through experiencing different ways of playing it we can explore the tone of these scenes. By this stage the actress playing Helena will have realized that there is a robust quality in the humour and playing of the mechanicals which does not belong to the lovers. Their scenes are full of life, but the humour comes more from situation than broadness of character. Improvisations will have shown that, though both groups take themselves seriously, there is a naïve delight in the mechanicals' approach which leads to the quality of humour they produce, while it is a naïve earnestness which makes us laugh at the lovers.

In present-day comedies which have come to be known as "comedies of menace" a similar problem of tone exists. It is sometimes difficult for the actor to grasp how much is comedy and how much menace. On the cold page or in a reading lines occur which seem most amusing, and may lead to the actor playing for comedy. It is not difficult, for instance, to see Ben in *The Dumb Waiter* as a comedian, and sometimes, viewed in isolation, the dialogue between Ben and Gus is highly comical. It is not until actors begin to move around with the situation that they begin to grasp that in context most of this "comedy" is overridden by the atmosphere of menace. We must sense Gus's agitation and the seriousness of it at the outset, so that we laugh as it were cerebrally, but the laughter is held back from being made audible, through the communication of fear. In *The Caretaker* the menace unfolds in a different way. It is there from the beginning with the way in which Mick sits on the bed. On the page it looks like this:

> Mick is alone in the room, sitting on the bed. He wears a leather jacket.
> Silence.
> He slowly looks about the room, looking at each object in turn. He looks up at the ceiling, and stares at the bucket. Ceasing, he sits quite still, expressionless, looking out front. Silence for thirty seconds.
> A door bangs. Muffled voices are heard.
> Mick turns his head. He stands, moves silently to the door, goes out, and closes the door quietly.

It is not easy to sense the significance of this from just looking at it in a book, but it is an important clue to the author's approach. Put Mick sitting on the bed in his leather jacket, and let him and those watching feel the silence. Give him the opportunity to stare up at the bucket and again sit "quite still, expressionless, looking out front". Again, feel the silence, this time for half a minute. This is a long time to watch an expressionless, motionless character at the beginning of a play, but this is how the mood is set. Davies comes in and is mildly amusing as a character, but the menace is there in the unknown character who went out almost before the play started. If actors can get at this kind of feeling in early preparatory work on a text, plays of this kind seem much less enigmatic and it is much more difficult to put the emphasis in the wrong places. The actor then knows how to approach his clipped interrogation of Davies at the beginning of Act 2, and understands in what kind of mood Mick handles the vacuum cleaner in the dark, in the second half of that act. In fact, as soon as actors become aware that the first impression of a play or scene may not be the best one, and become ready to explore and experiment through improvisation, the more likely they are to tune in to the style of comedy.

A good deal of time is often spent in the training of techniques and manners for period plays. However, given a text such as that

of a Restoration comedy it will usually be found that experiment
during improvisation on the play is a quicker approach. If groups
take, for instance, Congreve's *The Way of the World* and acquaint
themselves in the first instance with the plot line, as suggested in
the earlier stages of improvisation, if continued improvised work
is carried out using lace cuffs, Restoration skirts, sticks, quizzing
glasses, etc., the play will begin to develop a different form. Follow
this with work on a stage which attempts to give something of the
feeling of the period – as wings which give perspective, the small
apron stage, the proscenium arch, and an audience awareness will
add a further feeling for the style. Follow this with exploration of
the language of the play, working to capture the prose style of some
of the Millamant-Mirabelle scenes. Almost certainly, much of this
work is liable to send actors exploring aspects of the period, discovering more of the social history and so gradually building the
physical awareness of the period. This approach not only leads to
a deeper understanding of the kind of play with which we are
dealing, but it will also help us to see movement and manners as
part of character, costume and times, instead of a more abstract
isolated study. Similarly we can discover different styles of arti-
ficiality. The plays of Oscar Wilde can be seen more clearly in the
context of time and manners than if we try to understand them
solely from a reading, learning, acting point of view. The aristo-
cratic assurance and practised poise required for a play like *The
Importance of Being Earnest* are qualities which need to be explored
in a practical way rather than attempting to develop them after
being told about the style. Groups can improvise scenes involving
houses with space, carriages and servants and furniture of the
period, and discover remoter relationships involving an elaborate
set of unwritten rules and manners, growing to an understanding
of the kind of wit and verbal play which would accompany this
life.

When working on the plays of a writer like Chekhov groups
need to sense what is different in this author's writing from other
plays they might have met. Earlier work on, say, *The Three Sisters*,
in which they aimed to see the play as a whole, will have revealed
absence of obvious plot. It will quickly be appreciated, too, that
the dialogue which the author gives is in a dimension different from
the drama of previous times. Improvisations designed to discover
the style might begin with an attempt at acquaintance with the

characters. Here actors will find that for the reality of the play and its life they need to gain insight, and using the author's words as a starting-point explore in and around them.

The play begins with the three sisters, each in her own world. Olga is reminiscing about the day their father died, Masha is reading her book, and Irena is lost in her own thoughts. Let everyone at this early stage sense something of the inner life which leads to the words and attitudes which Chekhov gives. Other characters might be taken and worked on in this way. Then, as confidence is being gained in the sustained life of each character, they can begin to explore Chekhov's technique in what he makes the audience aware of. Take an Irena, Masha, Olga group and let them live through as much reality of their lives as they can at one part of the acting area, and introduce Toozenbach, Chebutykin and Soliony in another part of the stage. Then explore the focus of attention, shifting from one group into the other, until the ebb and flow of interest is an easy and natural one, yet the life of each group sustained and continuous. All through the play, other moments of this kind of attention-directing can be explored, so that the actors become familiar with the fact that the words which Chekhov gives us are simply the points of directed attention, while for the actor (and the audience's subconscious awareness) life goes on uninterrupted.

The contrasting approach of Brecht can then be seen to make different demands on the actor. He must come to a Brecht text without preconceptions of *the* acting approach. Instead, in working on a play like *The Caucasian Chalk Circle* it will soon be seen that the method is more one of illustrating a moral. Narrative and narrative illustration lie at the centre. Any suggestion of continuous life in the Chekhovian sense is soon put aside when we begin to improvise the relationship between the Story-teller or narrator and the participants in the acted scenes. Try acting the scene in which Grusha arrives at the peasant's cottage, seeking milk for the child, with its relationship to the Storyteller's words, and it is easy to feel that this world, though also taking isolated incidents, is taking them as illustration of a teaching point made, rather than as an example of life going on continuously. Improvisations taking moral tales or historical incidents and selecting scenes to be acted which illustrate an issue will help the actors to feel the different demands being made in their approach.

Brecht himself (*Brecht on Theatre*) suggests some improvisation exercises which include:

Dramatizing an epic. Passages from the Bible.
Situation: two women calmly folding linen. They feign a wild and jealous quarrel for the benefit of their husbands; the husbands are in the next room. They come to blows as they fold their linen in silence. The game turns serious.
Improvisation of incidents. Running through scenes in the style of a report, no text.

In all this work, aimed at the exploration of the kind of play and the author's approach, groups are learning to arrive at each text with an open mind and a sensitivity ready to tune into any one of a wide variety of styles. This extension of imagination and aware- ness enables actors to approach with confidence texts which at first seem difficult. When the exploratory work at the beginning shows that the text with which they are dealing relies to a great extent on a particular approach to language, actors will need to direct atten- tion on to the particular use of language with which the author presents them. It is surprising how quickly actors can absorb elements of verbal style through improvisation. Working, for instance, on Edward Albee's play *Who's Afraid of Virginia Woolf?* groups can take a page or two of the dialogue between George and Martha and explore it through reading it over first aloud and then, putting down the book, see what they can retain of these incisive interchanges. In the opening sequence, for instance, they can play over George's unwillingness to respond to Martha's incessant braying, and with a little observation and practice grasp the techniques he employs:

I haven't the faintest idea what . . .
I can't remember all the pictures . . .
What actor? What seat?

and then watch him rising to the attack when he discovers there is no peace. Building up the relationship between George and Martha gives actors the insight into the language used to convey the hidden battle, and soon they can find themselves in all kinds of situations, able to speak ideas or phrases which seem "pure George" or "pure Martha".

Or, faced with a play like *The Bald Prima Donna* by Ionesco

(Donald Watson's translation), and asked to present an improvised version, the only way of achieving any degree of success is to discover something of the technique which lies behind it. At first sight the last section, for instance, might seem without reason. Then, as it is worked on, patterns emerge and understanding dawns. Groups can achieve a mastery of the approach by learning how to create similar scenes or, taking the episode of the Fire Chief's visit, they might try making up stories on the same lines as some of the family narrative exchanges. Take for instance the Fire Chief's story:

> The Dog and the Ox. An experimental fable. Once upon a time, another ox asked another dog a question. Why haven't you swallowed your trunk? I beg your pardon, replied the dog, I always thought I was an elephant –

and then his:

> A young calf had eaten too much ground glass. As a result he had to be confined. He gave birth to a cow. But as the calf was a boy, the cow couldn't call him "mother". She couldn't say "father" to him either as he wasn't big enough. So the calf was obliged to get married to a certain young person, and the registry office made all the arrangements dictated by the current conventions.

The group can make the briefest notes on the main sections of the story and invent fables with a similar progression or take actual fables and give them a similar treatment. Then, if groups take Mrs Smith's "The Bouquet" or the Fire-Chief's "The Cold" and work on these in a similar way, they begin to see the relationship and can invent others with a different approach yet in the same idiom. They are now beginning to feel their way around this kind of narrative and use of language and are gaining confidence in the handling of the technique. Beginning with simple substitution, going on to simple parallels, we can develop the work to a highly imaginative level. All this creative work is contributing towards our understanding of the author and his play.

What the groups have been doing, in effect, in order to make these discoveries, is to put themselves in the author's shoes. They have acted his role in the creative process, in a way which will have afforded insight into his skill and manner of handling ideas, language and method of communication. Rather in the way in which they made discoveries about other people and human nature in general, by acting out situations and relationships, so here they have been making discoveries about the very nature of language and how men try to communicate, or avoid communicating, and seek to understand the complex impulses which surround it.

CHAPTER 16

Sensing the Shape and Rhythm

It is difficult adequately either to discover the shape of a play or discuss it using the printed page only. Shape involves elements of space, weight and time, and the written word can give us no more than a vague picture of this. Improvisation helps us to test out the feelings and impressions we have gathered from reading a text, and notice how variations affect the meaning and impact. In performance of a play, its length (that is, how long it takes to play), its pace (that is, the rate at which it is taken), are both affected by the elements of space (that is, where the action is imagined to take place) and the weight, or intensity, of the action. The interaction of these elements can best be seen by an illustration.

Shakespeare's *Coriolanus* begins in Rome, and moves in Act 1, scene 4, to Corioli, where the action remains for the next seven scenes. At the beginning of Act 2 the scene is Rome, where attention remains until Coriolanus's departure in Act 4, scene 1. From Act 4, scene 2, to the end of the play there is an alternation of attention between Rome and Antium, or wherever Coriolanus happens to be. So, from the point of view of place, some shape begins to merge which is best felt by a shortened improvised version of the play, designed to bring out this pattern:

Act 1, scenes 1–3	Mainly Rome
Act 1, scenes 4–10	Around Corioli
Act 2, scenes 1 to ⎫ Act 4, scene 1 ⎭	Rome
Act 4, scene 2 – end of play	Rome/Corioli

Groups are best left in the first instance to find their own solution to the presentation of place. Some may emphasize the change of locality, mainly through character, costume and dialogue. Others may find it clearer working through the use of different parts of the acting area. Props may help some or simply the change may be made apparent by a slight pause and a regrouping.

This space shape is affected or modified by the weight or emotional intensity. For instance, in Act 1 the first scene begins

with the discontented citizens meeting Menenius and Marcius. A
short scene follows when we see Aufidius with his senators. Then
the third scene takes us to the women, Volumnia and Virgilia,
which gives us the last of peaceful and domestic Rome. The
remaining scenes of this Act are a series of fighting encounters,
flowing one after the other, and rising to Marcius's final triumph
as Cominius gives him the title of Coriolanus. In scene 10 we see
something of the determination of the defeated Aufidius. So a kind
of texture shape is now seen:

Act 1, scene 1 Discontented yet domestic Rome ⎫ Preparatory-
Act 1, scene 2 Aufidius, the opposition   ⎬ emotional
Act 1, scene 3 The women talking of war   ⎭ undercurrent
Act 1, scenes 4–9 Fights, battles and encounters
   building to "Caius Marcius Coriolanus" –
   rising, more physically realized emotion
Act 1, scene 10. Determined Aufidius – emotional
   opposition kept alive.

Again, this is best understood by improvisation aimed to bring
out the emotional content. Groups can feel the intensity of the
beginning, which is quickly calmed by Menenius's speech. The
preparations at Corioli will then stand against this as a similar
emotional undercurrent played in a different place, while scene 3
presents the feminine emotional responses and prepares for the
contrasting build of the battle scenes.

Back to Rome for the next two acts: the texture is changed once
more and shaped by the peacetime election of a consul with all its
vicissitudes. Similarly, the texture of the last part of the play in
improvisation will be seen to add to the shape in its rhythmic
alternation between the anxious Romans and the impetuous Coriolanus.

In each of these elements of shape the time factor plays its part.
The crowd of citizens is effectively used to build an alternating
pattern of quicker pace which stands in contrast to a slower, calmer
rate of the scenes in which they do not appear. The improvisations
already carried out will have given some indication of this, but if we
work through part of the play with pace in mind we can see how
this is affected.

The effect of the citizens on the pace can be illustrated from
Act 3. In scene 1, the first section where Coriolanus is with the

senators indicates a fairly leisurely rate. Then the encounter with Brutus and Sicinius makes it move slightly faster, rising to the entry of the citizens, whose clamour takes it faster still. When the rabble is driven out the pace subsides, only to be revived on their re-entry. There is still a fairly intense atmosphere in the next scene, in the house of Coriolanus, but the whole tone is modified by the absence of the crowd. We feel them outside, as it were, but the pace moves more steadily during Coriolanus's alternation between refusing and deciding to return to them, cap in hand. In scene 3, the crowd again force the pace, and with it a heightening of intensity, even beyond the point at which Coriolanus turns his back. Similarly, the pace of their noise and acclamation stands in contrast to the slower scene of leave-taking with which Act 4 begins. This pace, acted out in improvisation, enables us to see the importance to the meaning and impact of the play of rhythmic shaping. The time length of the playing out of each phase of the play will also have its effect: a short scene followed by a long scene, followed by a further short episode, can only really be fully appreciated in its effect by living it in an atmosphere of time. In just the same way we appreciate the effect of spatial changes on the rhythmic modifications which occur when the scene which takes place in the market-place is followed by a scene indoors, followed by, say, a scene in the Forum.

Having discovered something of the overall shape of the play, groups can go on to exploring the rhythm of each scene which lies within this, and within the rhythm of each scene see the smaller rhythms and shape of each phase and speech. In *Coriolanus* this would mean improvised work aimed to explore such things as, in Act 2, scene 2, the preparation in which the two officers discuss Coriolanus's popularity and character, the change of pace and texture which occurs as the senators enter, the conflict added by the attitude of Sicinius and Brutus, Coriolanus's exit, Cominius's speech in praise of Coriolanus, Coriolanus's return, his greeting and almost immediately the return of the submerged conflict between him and Sicinius and Brutus, leading to Menenius's smoothing over the situation, and the final speeches leading us to realize that the tribunes intend to stir up the people. Each of these sections needs to be felt as an element in the physical shape which builds towards the overall impression of the scene. Each has its physical quality in respect of space relationships between the characters, each has its emotional intensity arising from degree and

kind of conflict, and each has its time, seen in the length of the
phase and its pace.

Groups can work upon all kinds of plays in this way, noting
through physical experience how in different plays now one element, now another, plays a more predominant part in the shaping.

In Ibsen's *Peer Gynt* perhaps the element which affects the
shape most is that of space. Groups improvising this will note
specially how Peer's travels work on the rhythm of the play. The
fact that we have so many shifts of scene from country to country
conditions the shape. On the other hand, the kind of locality of
any scene has its effect upon the rhythm. The movement from
mountainside and open air to the dark palace hall of the Troll
King, to pine forest, to the room in Peer's mother's house, to a
Morocco palm grove, to the desert, to Egypt, and so on, contribute
to the feeling of the play and understanding its impact. From the
cold page it is possible only to gather a vague idea of the way in
which these changes of locality and the comings and goings of the
characters alter or condition the play's effect, for it is not just that
the play changes from time to time, but what kind of changes these
are, which build the total effect.

It is easier to see after improvisations from a play like *Peer Gynt*
the completely different impact and conception of shape which is
achieved in a play which preserves unity of place. The Greeks used
their acting area to represent one place very like the one it was in
reality. The space relationship to the structure of the play is therefore provided entirely by actor-to-actor relationship. What builds
the rhythm in a play like Sophocles' *Oedipus at Colonus* is the
interspersing of choric odes between the episodes involving clash
of character. The Greeks had a strong physical understanding of
the drama and made these choric interludes change with, and
comment upon, the section before and after. For instance, the first
choric section which introduces the chorus of elders begins with a
note of question and uncertainty indicating that they are looking
for the one who is defiling the place, but by the time Theseus has
arrived the shape and texture of their words and movement has
gathered an intensity. When Creon and Theseus leave to investigate what has happened to Ismene and Antigone, the whole emotional tone rises and the chorus builds the audience response still
further through its shape and pattern. So we have the two main
elements working side by side in shaping this kind of play: the pace,

intensity and physical relationship of the meeting between the characters, broken at fairly regular intervals not just by a verbal comment, but by ideas expressed in physical movement, emotional intensity and pace. Improvised sections of such a play will help groups to appreciate the total relationship between actors and chorus in shaping the play.

In a modern play which also preserves unity of place, like Pinter's *The Dumb Waiter*, there is no chorus, but the shape of the play is governed by similar forces to those shaping Greek drama. It is not difficult to feel the intensity of the mood built into *The Dumb Waiter*, but it is interesting for groups to notice the way in which the pace factor works on the overall impression the play gives an audience. With a play like this the leader can give his groups an opportunity of experiencing the variety of pace working with emotional intensity. Things move slowly at the beginning as Ben reads the paper and comments. Gus's reactions break the incidents and here something of a chorus effect is provided by his anxious reiteration of the questions which are perplexing him. Later, the pace increases and the rhythm is affected by the unnerving rumble of the dumb waiter's descent on five separate occasions. Very soon groups will become aware of these and other elements. They will notice the effect that repetition of a line or action has at different points in the play and understand its purpose. They will begin to sense also the effect of the rhythm of interruptions in the action, whether provided by a narrator or chorus, a lighting change or an interval. These points will not remain as points outside their experience and control, but they will grow to see them as conditions affecting the play as a whole, and therefore their feeling for, and within, them.

It is worth spending some time focusing attention on the rhythm which lies in the speech and dialogue. It is easy to forget that here, too, rhythm has a physical quality and link. Even the terms used in speaking of rhythm in the line have a movement basis. We talk of metre and sometimes forget its physical length. We measure rhythm in feet and are apt to forget the dance quality. It is useful to give groups practice in learning to feel the rhythm of the speech as part of the beat of the character. Take, for instance, Jimmy Porter in *Look Back in Anger*. He likes words, enjoys them for their own sake, and delights in using his imagination in association with them:

> All this time, I have been married to this woman, this monument to non-attachment, and suddenly I discover that there is actually a word that sums her up. Not just an adjective in the English language to describe her with – it's her name! Pusillanimous!

Let groups take this speech as it stands and attempt to feel its rhythm and shape as they speak it aloud. Work for a time on the opening statements, until they begin to sense the slow measured pace with which it begins and the sarcasm of the phrase in apposition. Then let them join this on to the feeling of the growing impetus as the pace rises as Jimmy gleefully declares his "pusillanimous". Once people begin to feel the speech and its rhythmic pattern, they begin to feel the movement. It is almost impossible to deliver this standing still. The shape of the words demands movement. There is an aliveness in head and shoulders, arms and hands respond. Then continue with Jimmy's flight of fancy:

> It sounds like some fleshy Roman matron, doesn't it? The Lady Pusillanimous seen here with her husband Sextus, on their way to the Games. Poor old Sextus! If he were put into a Hollywood film, he's so unimpressive, they'd make some poor British actor play the part. He doesn't know it, but those beefcake Christians will make off with his wife in the wonder of stereophonic sound before the picture's over.

Give groups an opportunity of being carried away by the rhythmic drive of the rhetoric, a time or two, and then, working in threes, let one be Alison and the other Cliff, while Jimmy lets the speech and its shape make the physical relationship between himself and the other two. This approach is a means of working from the emotion of the passage and sensing the time and space links with the intensity. After working through the speech a few times in this manner, actors will find that even without the book or speech written in front of them, they will be using Osborne's words, and will begin to appreciate something of Jimmy's thought and speech power to an extent which will enable them to create speeches in character for situations not presented in the play.

When dialogue is an interchange, the rhythm is altered and affected by what happens between exchanges. It is important then to go on from working on single extended speeches to developing awareness of rhythm between the actors. The short lines used considerably in Samuel Beckett's *Waiting for Godot* need rhythmic experiment. In just a few lines, interpretation and impact can change with the pattern:

ESTRAGON: What do we do now?
VLADIMIR: While waiting?
ESTRAGON: While waiting
            (*Silence*)
VLADIMIR: We could do our exercises.

Let the actors play with the different effects to be gained by speaking this exchange at different rates and with varying amounts of pause. Try it with the first three lines spoken in rapid succession followed by a long pause broken by a slow "We could do our exercises". Then take them at a medium rate, with an enthusiastic speaking of Vladimir's line. Try it again with a pause after Estragon's first line and so on, noticing how the rhythm and expression affect the meaning, both conscious and subconscious. Then add the next lines:

ESTRAGON: Our movements.
VLADIMIR: Our elevations.
ESTRAGON: Our relaxations.
VLADIMIR: Our elongations.
ESTRAGON: Our relaxations.
VLADIMIR: To warm us up.
ESTRAGON: To calm us down.
VLADIMIR: Off we go.

Immediately the actors will realize another element affecting the shape, for we not only have lines each of two words in length, but we also have similar sounds occurring. Each begins with a lightly stressed syllable and from "elevations" to "relaxations" we have words all ending in "ations" and of the same number of syllables. Take the whole sequence at this point and explore its pattern throughout. Play about with not just the words but the characters speaking the words. Let them in turn be enthusiastic, then dejected, then noncommittal, then uncertain, and at times vary the mood throughout the sequence. Let the actors take the sequence sitting down, quite still; standing up; moving about; and all kinds of shades of meaning will result. In the end the sequence has to be seen in its context in the play as a whole. One shape and rhythm of this sequence will very probably add more to the overall interpretation of the play which the group felt best and most effective in earlier explorations.

Even where the dialogue may appear to be more prosaic, a sense of rhythm and shape can considerably affect the impact it has upon both actors and audience.

Look at the following extract from Act 2 of *The Knack* by Ann Jellicoe:

COLIN: Let's go look for the Y.W.
NANCY: Are you coming?
TOLEN: To the Y.W.?
COLIN: Well, let's you and me go.
NANCY: Well –
COLIN: Well –
NANCY: I don't think I really –
COLIN: You said you did.
NANCY: Did I?
COLIN: Yes.
NANCY: What about the cases?
TOLEN: Why don't you carry them?
COLIN: Me?
TOLEN: If you're going to the Y.W., why don't you carry them?

If you try speaking this, either alone or with others, changing the tempo, the moments of pause, the moments of emphasis, it is interesting to see how the pattern affects the meaning and impact of this section of the scene. In early stages it is useful to underline the rhythm of such a passage with a drum beat, later picking it up with a hand clap. We can try varying the enthusiasm of Colin's "Well, let's you and me go". The two "Well – " spoken by Nancy and then Colin might repeat the same strength of beat, or they can be given a different weight, depending on the degree of interest shown. When we have mastered a certain rhythmic shape we can begin to attempt the building of the same shape, using different words. All this is tuning the ear, and training aural sensitivity, so that in plays which have a more obvious verse form the actor does not find himself less at home. The same principles apply in Shakespeare, where we need to feel the emotional drive of the verse, and not be ready to analyse it according to an anglicized version of a Greek verse, though originally dance measure. Once we are sensitive to the rhythm with all its changes and variations, we can feel the skill of the dramatist as he moves from one mood into another, with an alteration of the verbal pattern. In just these few lines which take us from the murder of Duncan to the Porter's letting in of Macduff, we can feel the night passing into the morning:

LADY MACBETH: . . . Hark! more knocking.
  Get on your nightgown, lest occasion call us,
  And show us to be watchers. – Be not lost
  So poorly in your thoughts.
MACBETH: To know my deed, 'twere best not know myself.
  Wake Duncan with thy knocking: I would thou couldst!
PORTER: Here's a knocking indeed! If a man were porter of
  hell-gate, he should have old turning the key.

Here, even in broad daylight, and with no change of lighting, actors responding to the rhythm can convey to the audience a great deal on the emotional plane. Continuity is preserved, but the change in the shape of the play cannot fail to be observed by all. Actors need opportunity to be able to work on all these rhythms and to understand how one actor's exit or entrance affects the coming or going of another.

CHAPTER 17

Meeting and Knowing the Characters

The elements we have so far been experiencing have been mainly concerned with the play as a whole. It cannot be too strongly emphasized that for whatever purpose one is approaching the text the total view of the play must come first, and it is only when we have come to grasp something of all these other aspects that we should turn our attention towards the characters. If the actor can be persuaded to come to the part he is playing after acquainting himself with the play, he is likely to find that his approach is quicker and deeper and generally more effective. The tendency is too often to start straight away on the study of the character to be played and to limit one's sights in this direction. If improvisation has been the main approach, it is already likely that he will have experienced several other parts and so understand the needs and relationships much better.

The first approach to a single character must be to discover his function in the play, for every characterization must be created with reference to his purpose. Every part needs life and impact, but due regard will need to be paid to the relationship to other characters, to the scene, and to the play as a whole. Throughout the building of a character it is helpful if groups can work on each other's roles so that everyone can have an opportunity of seeing the character he is to interpret played by at least one other person. In this way he can see the dangers and the difficulties and perhaps gain insight into the situation by being able to stand outside as well as inside his shoes. We have seen that the two basic ways in which we as human beings make discoveries from earliest childhood onwards are to live out a role gaining a vicarious experience, and to put someone else in our place, so that we can look objectively at even our own situation.

Much of the work suggested in our earlier discussion on character building can be applied here, this time referring back to the text instead of our imaginations for the detail. Basically, we need to approach improvisations and the text with a number of questions:

I.   What does the character do when he is alone?
II.   What does he do when he is with others?
III. What does he say when he is alone?
IV.   What does he say when he is with others?
V.   What do others say about him?
VI.   How do others treat him?
VII. How does he generally respond to others?

In all this there is a need to evaluate how far we should accept surface manifestations, and how far these should be modified in the light of what we know about the situation. We need to be aware also of the kind of play the character appears in.

Let us take a look at some of the different ways in which playwrights have built characters and see the kind of improvisations which might result from creating a character in plays of each sort. There are many plays in which the writer creates a character with a good deal of background supplied. Improvisation does not, as we have made clear, mean that one does not have to study the text, but rather that, out of a practical approach, we find the need to utilize all that lies within. Shakespeare abounds with characters richly drawn, and Prince Hal in *Henry IV*, *Part I* will illustrate some ways in which such a character might be explored.

The tavern will be the starting-point, where scenes of Hal with Falstaff can be improvised, trying to capture something of their verbal fencing. Actors will discover from this something of the Prince's regard for Falstaff and Falstaff's regard for the Prince. Groups can build scenes with these two, Gadshill, Poins, and the rest and scenes in which the company are without Falstaff. They can then work on the Prince–Poins relationship and try to capture something of the easier interchange of words between them. They can plan not only the Gadshill robbery but also other escapades in which they enjoy a joke at Falstaff's expense. Living in and out of the tavern sequences it is possible to capture something of the gusto of their impromptu play-making, and by regularly leaving the Prince to himself after each of these scenes see other qualities and moods at work.

Then the groups can explore the Prince at court, meeting the young Hal with his father at the famous interview, and at other times build scenes in which he avoids the court, but realizes nevertheless his responsibility. At some stage, it might be as well

if he played scenes in Hotspur's shoes, so that he can understand
in what ways he is a contrast to him, and so that when he refers to
him he does so with more than verbal understanding. Finally, when
he comes to meet him on the battlefield he can give him the full
spirit of the encounter, and speak his praise with greater understanding.

Such scenes will reveal all kinds of points for discussion and
show points of difficulty or apparent inconsistency which can be
solved not in theory but through experience.

With a character like Hal we have much on which to work, and
the task may well seem at first sight to be more interesting than the
creating of character where the author has deliberately battened
upon one facet of human nature. Usually, however, a closer look
will reveal subtlety of presentation and nearly always improvisations will enable the actor to discover opportunities for varying the
texture which will serve, and not detract from, the text.

With his theory of humours, Ben Jonson presents us with a host
of single-trait characters. Generally, too, the trait for portrayal is
clearly expressed even in the name. In *Volpone*, for instance, we
have the fox, Mosca the fly, Corvino the crow, Corbaccio the raven,
and even Sir Politick Would-Be. All advertise their central characteristic. If groups were to build, say, Voltore the vulture, it would
be as well to look, in the first instance, to find out about the bird
with whose name Jonson has christened the advocate.

Something of these discoveries about the creature can help in
creating the physical presence of the character: the hooked beak
and repulsive appearance, and its abnormally keen senses of sight
and smell. These two last characteristics might form the beginnings
of improvised scenes, for Voltore thinks he can tell when death is
near. Like the bird, however, he will not touch the carcass until it is
quite dead, but hovers by. Actors can improvise on the interviews
which he has with Volpone and work, too, upon his relationship
with Mosca, the fly. A group might devise scenes outside Volpone's
house to bring out the relationship between him and the other
birds of prey, showing their distrust and envy of each other, yet
each responding in his own characteristic manner. Each of these
characteristics and discoveries can be linked with the fact that
Voltore is an advocate, where again his beak and eyes will play
their part, and his keenness in what he desires. Improvised scenes
can be built on Volpone's being brought to the senate house, but

we can also discover how he would conduct himself at other investigations and with other advocates. Discoveries like these will help to make the acting richer in nature, and yet, because actors are returning frequently to the text, they are ensuring that all is in accordance with Jonson's aim and direction.

When it is the task to create a character given by Brecht we can again recognize a different approach. Brecht is less concerned with the detail of background of a character and more with his reactions in a series of changing situations. He wants actor and audience to make up their minds about the character's behaviour. Improvisations will therefore be shaped to emphasize behaviour as well as aiding the necessary dexterity required to bring out the changing age and condition. In the building of a character like Galileo we might bring out at once the two sides of the man we find in scene 1: Galileo the researcher and questioner, and Galileo the opportunist. Other improvisations can establish his attitude towards the aristocracy and his feeling that he is kept impoverished while fools make money for squander. In other improvisations his relationship with, and attitude towards, the Church might be explored. This would bring out the power of the Church and show something of the dilemma in which some of its members found themselves. Galileo could gain insight into the relationship of himself with Andrea, Segrado and others by an interchange of parts, so each of the players would see the way all contributed to the build of the scenes. Further insight might be gained by improvising the first and last scenes one after the other, or by placing one after the other the scene in which he is at the height of his fame and the scene during which he renounces his teaching. It will help him, no doubt, to play out in full his trial and to improvise his secret working on the *Discorsi*. Further confidence and understanding of the character might be derived from improvisations aimed at developing the actors' use and knowledge of the models involved in his work. Useful scenes can also be devised with Andrea and his other pupils actually finding out about the heavens, and examining the night sky under differing conditions. In order to keep something of the Brechtian detachment, he can watch others developing his role and discuss the situations of the play both within and outside the context.

More recent plays by other authors working from a different standpoint also present characters without any obvious background. Some characterizations clearly call for greater penetration into psychological make-up. Working on the role of Davies in *The Caretaker*, the concern would be less where he went to school and what kind of a home he had than on understanding his particular temperamental make-up. The text, of course, abounds in intellectual clues, but the aim of rehearsals would be to capture his particular outlook. After some exploration of the changing relationship between Davies and Aston, the actors might go on to scenes between Mick and Davies and try to discover the man's intuitive handling of each of the brothers. Davies needs to gain lots of practice in the speech idiom and to feel phrases and imagery which make the character rich. Physically, too, the understanding of the man can be developed by feeling what shoes and socks, overcoat and trousers, shirt, vest and so on, contribute to making the man. Davies can talk a good deal to himself in his attempt to come to terms with the outside world of reality and the "would-be", "if-only" world in which he lives. He can build up, too, a collection of all the grievances he has against society and all its members, and observe his immediate world, discovering ways in which it could serve his purposes. He can also feel the contrast of his tentative, uncertain beginning with his gradual increase of confidence and daring. He must explore in scenes with Mick and Aston his ever-shifting diplomacy in the light of any given situation.

Such improvisations and his earlier work on the play will help him to decide on the kind of character he is interpreting, and whether he can best serve the play by acting for humour or pathos, or being aware of the menace.

Many actors, called upon to play the smaller part, feel especially tempted to deal only with the few lines which the author has given them to say. Where there is a genuine group feeling it is much more possible to sustain the overall interest in someone portraying a short role, and if time has been spent with the group as a whole working on the entire play, this is found to be of value to all concerned. Furthermore, if in rehearsals when characterization is the focus frequent changes of role are undertaken, then this becomes much more than a mere means of holding the company's interest, and actors begin to see how everyone can make a contribution to the understanding of the central characters. This will help to ensure that the small character part fully realizes why he enters and what exactly the contribution of that entry, and the lines spoken, really is.

Susanna Wolcott, for example, in *The Crucible*, comes in to speak only four short speeches in Act 1. From the lines she has to say, and those spoken to her, we can gather a good deal about the immediate situation. But she needs to understand her part in the summoning of spirits in order to give her visit to the Rev. Parris's its proper mood. She should work with Abigail and the other girls to establish clearly the night they were discovered by Parris, and to help everyone to grasp the power involved. This will not make her part any larger, but it will ensure that her acting of it is meaningful to her and the audience, even though, perhaps, in the case of the audience, it does no more than strike the correct preparatory note.

Characters who have nothing at all to say appear for long periods in some plays and their characters require just as careful building as any of the others. The deaf and blind Helen Keller in *The Miracle Worker* is an exacting part, and the Japanese prisoner in *The Long and the Short and the Tall* remains the centre of most of the action for almost two-thirds of the play. In Pinter's *A Slight Ache* the match-seller has nothing to say, has no background, no clear appearance or characteristics, and yet he dominates the entire atmosphere. In a play such as this the group needs to work on many scenes in which characters dominate and are dominated, both with and without words. Power and menace of presence can be experimented upon, discovering ways in which this can be achieved. The three characters can each in turn try scenes in which one of them is completely still or constantly moving, in which the body is the force of power, through its sheer aliveness, or through its absolute deadness. They can work on scenes in which the eyes are the central interest, either because of their fixed stare, in an unfocusing way, or because of their ever-present penetration.

We are told that the man is a match-seller and we can work on scenes which explore facets of this occupation and the physical condition – the tray, the string and the boxes, and what such paraphernalia can do to a person, or the person can do to it. Such items as the smile on his lips or his crying can be taken up, and the kind of expression which can appear to be changing without doing so. The actor needs to be aware of what he can contribute and how he can detract. It would be useful, too, if all the characters could spend some time on working on facial expressions in a mirror, observing especially the qualities of eyes and mouth. The actor playing the match-seller needs to understand the whole shape of the play if he is to make the right contribution. Silent he may be, but he must be eloquent.

Irrespective of size of character in either lines or moments of appearance, the treatment is a similar one. We first of all gather a fair amount of detail from the text and then work on it in improvised form in both the actual situations from the play and imagined ones. These will send groups back to the text for further understanding, so that building of character is based on the accuracy and clarity of the improvised work. The characterization will continue to grow and will remain alive, while the actor keeps feeling and thinking, and thinking and feeling.

CHAPTER 18

Creating the Atmosphere

There are two particular uses of improvisation in connexion with the atmosphere of a play; the first is a means of exploration of the atmosphere, and the second is in developing this mood.

The atmosphere of a play exists in its emotional content, and as this builds in the rhythmic shaping of the drama we rise to moments of great height or intensity – the climaxes. Again, it is easy to see how much the atmosphere of the play is a physical condition built up by relationships between people or between a person and his imagination, or between a person and the physical world. It is possible to realize something of this in reading, but nearly always living it out modifies or heightens the mood.

Some plays have a quite definite atmosphere which pervades the play throughout. In many of Ibsen's plays there is quite a strong mood which remains throughout the drama. *Rosmersholm*, *Lady from the Sea*, and *Ghosts* each have their ever-present mood. Similarly, in the plays of Chekhov, although we are dealing with a quite different texture, something of the mood established in the early scenes of, say, *The Cherry Orchard* or *Uncle Vanya* remains throughout, so that in all these cases it is important for work of both exploration and establishing the atmosphere to be carried out.

Early reading of *The Three Sisters* will give a clue to elements which help to establish the atmosphere. One is clearly associated with reminiscing, looking back to earlier times and recalling them with considerable detail and vividness, and improvisations can develop this element. We can explore how this is built into the contrasting feelings of the upsurge of desire to do something vigorous and the inability to carry it through. Other themes will quickly suggest themselves and can be related to the sense of period and aristocracy.

With Arthur Miller's *The Crucible*, we have to capture the austerity of the religious life in Salem in 1692, so that improvisations can be carried out to bring home the strictness of things like Sunday observance, standards of sexual conduct, authority of the Bible and consequently of church leaders. We can work also on the feeling of the close-knit community, in which everyone knows and is known. Other things to sense in improvisation are the complete absence in such a community of any type of entertainment or enjoyment and the strong belief in, on the one hand, a God with a strict sense of justice and, on the other, a devil with a cunning which must be dealt with in the most ruthless way. Improvisations would deal with the everyday round of such people, their rising in the morning, their farmwork, their mealtimes, their church-going and sermons. Into this, groups can begin to build a sense of character and the subtleties of human nature which give us the Abigails, the Titubas, and the Proctors. In this way, when it comes to building the mood of hysteria of Act 3 or the solemnity and depression of Act 4, it can be seen to rise out of this overall atmosphere of Salem village.

At other times, instead of one strongly present atmosphere running right through the piece, we are given two or more contrasts of mood. In a play like *The Royal Hunt of the Sun* by Peter Shaffer this arises from the meeting of two distinct worlds. Spanish adventurers invade the sanctity of South American Indians. Such a contrast quite frequently occurs in Shakespeare, where two or more plots are being built alongside each other. In *Henry IV, Part I*, the tavern world is set alongside that of the court. In *The Merchant of Venice*, Belmont is set against commercial Venice, and perhaps one of the clearest and best examples is in *A Midsummer Night's Dream*, where three worlds, each with its own atmosphere, exist throughout the play. The way of building these atmospheres as separate entities is to work as the company did in *The Royal Hunt of the Sun*, so that the different worlds rehearse apart, under their different leaders creating their own appropriate mood. Prospero's world in *The Tempest* can be improvised with one group in one place: theirs is an island of strange noises and creatures, controlled by one master creator. They can build scenes involving the different levels of spirits – spirits of the air and atmosphere, like Ariel, Iris, Ceres, and others, living alongside the spirits of earth, like Caliban. This will enable Miranda to know her island, not just in name but also in feeling, so that she learns how really cut off she is from the rest of humanity. In another area Alonso, Sebastian, Antonio, Ferdinand, Gonzalo and so on work on scenes involving a world of the aristocracy and politics. So, before the time comes for these characters to leave Italy, there has already been built a mood of rivalry and intrigue. As a kind of subdivision of this world, or a world within a world, we might build the comic kingdom of Stephano and Trinculo. These two, then, meeting on the island, have a background of living experience and understanding on which to draw, and so their meeting with Caliban comes as a meeting with a kindred spirit in a strange world of magic. Even before they leave Italy they, too, feel their position in relation to their masters, and already look with some envy upon power and luxury. With this kind of approach we establish clearly the two worlds and help to keep the life of the mixture of the two atmospheres at points where they are interwoven.

There is, however, in some plays much more of a contrast existing, where one mood is established only to be broken by another, or at other times one mood falls over into another. In many of the comedies of Shakespeare the buoyant feeling of comedy is pierced by elements of tragedy (e.g. Shylock's doom in *The Merchant of Venice*, Malvolio's parting at the end of *Twelfth Night*). In a play like *Juno and the Paycock* the comedy is limited to the first two acts and tragedy appears in Act 3. We have already discussed a little about *The Infernal Machine*, and here, too, we have a light-hearted approach in one act which is replaced by tragedy and even horror later in the play.

Henry Livings has given us an insight in several of his plays into a close relationship between farce and pathos and near-tragedy. In *Stop It, Whoever You Are* he establishes ludicrous situations in which the characters act with the broad quality of farce, then before we quite realize it the action has gained a new dimension and we are responding in a situation full of pathos. At the end of the play, when Warbeck has become a rather pathetic character with whose misfortune we feel involved, the mood is dextrously switched back into the world of farce. All this requires practice and exploration on the part of the group working on the play. They can devise situations which involve real characters responding in a realistic situation, and meeting misfortune – the sort of situation we have in *Stop It, Whoever You Are*, for instance, when Warbeck finds himself tempted by Marilyn Harbuckle – and these can be developed on a serious level. The same scene can then be played on a completely different level, working purely on the comedy or farce of the situation, or we can take situations from other plays which have a serious mood, and build instead a much more light-hearted relationship. For instance, there is a nice contrast already evident in the different treatments of a father's ghost in the beginning of *Hamlet* and in the beginning of Cocteau's *The Infernal Machine*.

As the group becomes used to being able to work clearly in the building of each mood they might then work on scenes in which the atmosphere changes both gradually and abruptly from one world into the other.

Closely linked with this approach to atmosphere is the approach to comedy generally. Playing without an audience a play which is at heart a comedy can be a difficult business, and usually the actors find themselves working in the dark, until they feel the audience response on the first night. The advantage in these situations of group work and of one group playing to another in rehearsals will enable the actors to test out something of what seems to come across and what does not. It also enables them to test timing and helps the group to feel the comedy inherent in good teamwork. Alan Aykbourn has written an ingenious comedy, *Mr Whatnot*, built largely upon the use of an amplified sound track, running parallel with the action which is mainly mimed. It would not be surprising to find that this play, in fact, had grown out of improvised work, and certainly a good deal of the business would grow from trial and error in rehearsals. The hilarious scene in which Mr Whatnot vanishes under the table, spending most of his time transferring wine glasses from one end of the dinner-table to the other, lends itself to exploration through improvisation. Comedy, above all, calls for invention to keep the play living and spontaneous, and all kinds of discoveries can be made, where groups are continually sharing their work with other groups in the rehearsal time. Even when the play itself is being run through for the sake of continuity and timing, a freshness of approach can be maintained by giving it a different dimension, such as that of playing it as melodrama, or in cod American, Chinese, or the like.

With some plays it is difficult to find any tangible atmosphere, or maybe the atmosphere exists in there being no apparent atmosphere at all. Beckett's *Waiting for Godot* can be explored from this point of view. Estragon and Vladimir exist in their place, which is no place, and carry out a series of actions, which are no actions. If, as well as sensing the rhythm of their language and lives, the actors also improvise, building on the idea of waiting in a situation which is out of time, they begin to build a sense of the mood of the piece, their words and actions go on in this no-man's-land, penetrated only by Pozzo and Lucky and the boy. In a similar way, Pozzo and Lucky build their world as a separate atmosphere, again existing nowhere, and going no place in particular. It is only the boy who seems to have any sense of immediate purpose, coming from a place of atmosphere and returning to it. Out of this combination of pause, apparently insignificant action, and short philosophical exchange, they build the void which through time rises to a power which reaches a point of being almost unbearable. Or, to put it another way, they are, in fact, getting rid of time, place and obvious human emotion, to establish the aching emptiness which lies at the centre of the play.

The atmosphere in Pinter's plays, though still not tangible, is one of which we are more clearly aware. Menace grows through his plays, in one form or another. In *The Dumb Waiter* and in *The Birthday Party* the emotion is heightened by the use of sound. The dumb waiter rumbles and clatters into an already tense and nervous situation. The toy drum builds its rhythms to increase the menace and darkness backs this up in *The Birthday Party*. Working on either of these plays, we can explore the emotional qualities of sounds, and work on scenes in which sinister and mysterious characters, both absent and present, came into the world. There is also good opportunity in these plays for the working up of small fears through a sense of guilt and our own imagination, into the powerful threats they become. Catechism and ritual and cross-examination can be developed in the building of atmosphere, and we can work out in rehearsal the different effects obtained by going through these routines, in a soft insistent voice, in firm commanding tones, slowly, or with pace and in different physical relationships.

Perhaps amongst the most difficult atmospheres to create are those which exist in situations which by now have become rather hackneyed. Shakespeare abounds with scenes which have been "done to death" and Shaw has some notable examples of everybody's favourites. In cases like these we have to try to take a fresh look at the mood and divorce it from traditional associations. It is very difficult to see anything like a satisfactory production of *Macbeth*, and this may partly be due to the fact that we have become much too familiar with the witches. Cauldrons, smoke, pointed hats, hooked noses and so on tend to block us from any impact these characters might make. Suppose then, instead, we work on the whole attempt at trying to understand man's present life in relation to the future, and we do some improvisations working on various ways in which man has tried to see beyond his present moment. Gradually, we can feel the opposition of the Church, and of society, and feel our characters being cast out of the towns into the less-inhabited areas of moor and marshland. Alongside this, we might work on the power of one man or woman over another, and explore images and effigies. Then, when we have grasped something of the representational method of gaining control, we can discover man's attempt to bring power through language and the use of spell. We can experiment with chiming, rhyming words, and as we did under the section on rhythm, develop the power of the regular beat and find something of its hypnotic grip and mystery. While in these investigations try out rhythmic sound patterns made with the voice, nonsense sounds or use of foreign language, especially Latin, or any sound associated with either great learning or religion. This can take us back to a fresh look at the opening scene of *Macbeth*, noting the added grappling with the unknown in the elements.

Rhythm and mood-wise, this opening scene can be played against the other scenes, noting how the mood changes and with it the rhythmic and emotional undertones, and by breaking or varying the rhythm at certain places it is possible to build a strong association of the witches with the powers beyond man's reach.

It sometimes happens that the mood of a particular scene escapes a group of actors because it is really outside their experience, and it is here that we need to look for some equivalent within their experience which will help to start them on the imaginative bridge to the scene being worked on. For young modern actors brought up in a welfare state, it is happily hard for them to understand hunger, so that if called upon to play, for instance, the opening scene of *Coriolanus*, their acting may lack the fervour and urgency in their feelings towards the patricians. We would need in this case to devise some means of bringing such a grievance near the realms of possibility. We might try, in the first instance, complaints about the quality of food in the canteen. This can lead to the realization that there is food available, but that "they" are getting it all. Most of us feel stirred when it comes to demanding our rights, and tempers rise when authority seems to be living in ease and comfort while we are getting less than our due. In many scenes parallels of this kind can be found and will usually be sufficient to spark off the necessary emotional understanding.

Finally, notice the building of an atmosphere conditioned by something which takes place "off-stage". It is generally very difficult to stand on any stage and look out into the wings or audience and describe something in such a way that the event taking place outside builds a real sense of atmosphere amongst the actors present. Ibsen in *Rosmersholm* gives Mrs Helseth a particularly difficult task in making her look from the window and describe Rosmer and Rebecca leaping into the mill-stream. It is with this that the play closes, and up to that moment the housekeeper has had comparatively little to do. Also at this point of the play she has little opportunity to prepare herself. Unless she can make the off-stage event have reality for herself, she will fail to build anything or communicate anything for the audience.

With *The Master Builder* the situation is even more difficult, for Mrs Solness, Dr Herdal, Ragnor, Hilda and several other ladies are all standing watching Solness climb the tower off-stage. Here it is important that not only should every one of them have a vivid impression of the master builder's climb and his fall to destruction, but that every one of them should experience this at the same time. The group can try working upon small things to begin with and building up to larger demands upon their imagination and emotional response.

Supposing we begin with an actual spider, which can build some feeling among the ladies especially, and go on to, say, a mouse and a rat and a wild animal (in the imagination!) aiming each time to keep the unity of response and building to a moment of climax. (Some of the exercises in Chapter 10 may be appropriate.) They can work on looking into a pit, or a hole in the road, where the definition of the space is again clear. Then, they can develop this into things taking place through a window or a door, building up to a disaster on a high building. Let them try differing emotional responses, say, a tight-rope walker fooling about, causing a snatch of breath, and finally a disaster, and in each case encourage individual response and characterization within the group unity of timing. If they are working on *The Master Builder* it can help if the group can actually see their Solness standing precariously on a high scaffolding or building, so that there is some assurance that all have a similar visual focal point which they can carry in imagination through performances. With the building of mood and atmosphere in rehearsal, and the awareness of rhythm and shaping, the groups will readily feel the moments of greatest tension, ensuring that, in performance, each member of the company contributes to an effective climax.

CHAPTER 19

Making Reports Real

It is one of the easiest tasks in the world to present a long speech of reporting with flatness. The difficulty, as elsewhere, is to make the words live, or to make them part of the person who is speaking them. It is slightly less of a problem when a character is simply reporting something which is supposed to have happened to him, though even here some difficulty is still present. When one is reporting what one has seen, as a moderately disinterested on-looker, or what one has been told, as a mere message-conveyer, it is particularly hard to make a vast amount of words have meaning and life. Especially is this so when those words are not, in fact, ours, but are presented to us on the page. So although we shall try to work on different approaches, the aim is always the same; to bring the words to the conscious mind and make the thoughts and the language in which those thoughts are expressed have meaning and reality.

The whole of this is linked with the oldest of arts, that of telling a story, and we can all enjoy practice in narrating the gist of the film we have seen or a book we have read, or an incident which may have happened to us. Working in groups, the aim is to make the narrative live to an extent which will make the audiences retain all the essential evidence, and then the story can be retold by some of those who have been listening. Actors can work on the carrying of a message from one person to another; beginning with a statement of no special consequence, they can go on to the reporting of grave news like the death or illness of a relative, national disasters, the result of a battle, and so on, varying each time the relationship between the teller and the person receiving the news, so each time the manner of telling will change, but the important thing will be to make the message clear both to those who are receiving the news and those who are in the audience. This leads to work calling for a greater awareness of the response from the person or persons to whom the actors are reporting, and then to scenes in which the news is received, causing distress to the recipient, causing anger, causing joy, and so on. The messenger may at times be aware of the effect the message will have, and at other times be surprised by this.

The messenger in Greek tragedy has always an onerous task involving two or three pages, very often, of detailed description of what has taken place in relation to the chief character. He may be reporting violence or destruction or sadness, but he needs to make the scene as clear as he can. He must decide how much participation the piece demands, and if his job is to remain rather as an impartial observer, he can still be aware of the fact that he is a human being who might be impressed or alarmed by the scene. If at some stage the main elements of what he has to describe can be enacted imaginatively by the members of the group so that he can live out his messenger part, this will help. He can, in fact, direct this enactment of the off-stage scene, and this should help him to make sure that he has clarified in his own mind the details that are involved. It would also help him to realize which items are most important and need highlighting in his narration, and which are the colourful details which help to make the story as a whole vivid.

In Sophocles' *Oedipus at Colonus* the messenger returns to report the last moments of the life of the blind old Oedipus. He begins with the words, "It was wonderful", so that at the outset he prepares us for the fact that he responded to the scene and sets the tone for his description. The whole of the speech will in this mood need to be spoken with a reverent slowness, but the messenger still has to work on variety within this, and clear pointing will be required. He will discover from the practical work that the first paragraph or section deals largely with the description of the place, moving in the next phase to a narration of Antigone and Ismene clinging sorrowfully to their father. The peak of the mood of the piece comes in the next paragraph with his description of the voice. There is no need for him to attempt to imitate this, for it is clearly beyond all mimicry, but the words he uses to describe the situation and his reporting in direct speech mean that the listener should be left with a very clear impression:

. . . suddenly a voice called him, a terrifying voice at which all trembled and hair stood on end. A god was calling to him, "Oedipus! Oedipus!" it cried, again and again. "It is time: you stay too long." He heard the summons and knew that it was from God.

The rest of the speech follows a much quieter descriptive line. The drama is over and though "in what manner Oedipus passed from this earth no one can tell", the mood is one of serenity and assurance and the final sections are spoken with clarity and firmness.

There are times, however, when reporting is to describe not action but a scene. Enobarbus gives Antony a vivid description of the barge with Cleopatra regally sitting amidst the splendour, and although he is impressed he does not need to repeat the famous speech like a set piece at an audition. He is, after all, reporting something he has seen, and in improvisations he can take other members of the group on an imaginary tour of the barge, or help in its building and decoration. The important thing is that each of the comparisons should be spoken by him as if it came, in the first instance, from his imagination.

It is important for other characters in a play very often to be aware of a reported speech when they are involved in the narrative. Cleopatra would do well to accompany Enobarbus on his tour of the barge, and in Mary Warren's description of the day's events in Act 2 of *The Crucible* the rest of the girls and the judges can derive a great deal from re-enacting the trial of Goody Osburn. We can also improvise the scenes in which Goody Osburn came to the Proctors' household "beggin' bread and a cup of cider", and the mumbling the old woman made as she was turned away empty-handed. The later trial of Elizabeth Proctor will gain in its relevance if we work on the scene in which she was "somewhat mentioned". In the same act Cheever narrates the story of Abigail Williams at dinner in the Reverend Parris's house and how she fell to the floor screaming and was discovered to have a needle stuck two inches in her belly. Occurring as it does in Act 2, when neither Parris nor Abigail appear, it can go less observed and realized, but if it is enacted the incident can make its impact on all concerned and play its proper place in building the mood of Salem. It will also give insight into the way Abigail can develop her influence.

Arthur Miller makes his descriptions clear enough: the incidents are accurately described and presented with a richness of detail, but it sometimes happens that incidents are reported in other authors which leave us in doubt as to what actually took place. A case in point is the argument between Soliony and the Baron in the last act of *The Three Sisters*. Koolyghin tells us only, "It was outside the theatre . . . Soliony started badgering the Baron, and he lost patience and said something that offended him." Yet the incident is part of the life of the Baron and needs to be understood by him if the character is to live fully and the under-text remain alive. A scene can be set up in which Soliony and the Baron are leaving the theatre. There are many people round them and they will have to decide what it is they have seen. It is at this point that Soliony begins his badgering and he will have to find a reason for badgering him. Exchanges will follow, out of which the consequent loss of patience develops. Other characters will be embarrassed or enjoy the situation or half understand it, but all will be back to the text, looking for clues regarding their position, and making decisions in their test of reality.

Similarly, so many references in this and other plays of Chekhov can be explored in the improvised situation and given a meaning and understanding, which will ensure that the lines become more than just words and refer to aspects of the lives of the characters.

Apparently less-rewarding moments are sometimes found at the beginnings of plays, where two servants meet and talk about the people in the play whom none of us have so far met and so at this stage can have very little feeling for. Shakespeare presents us with such a situation at the beginning of *Cymbeline*. Ibsen does this in *The Wild Duck*, and Sheridan in *The Rivals* gives Fag and Thomas a large slice of atmosphere and character introduction. The producer and company can no doubt devise ways of adding life to the proceedings by introducing the characters as they are spoken about, or in some other visual way emphasizing what is being described. Above all, however, the descriptions themselves and the comments made need to have a life of their own for the characters reporting. Both Fag and Thomas have a character and a trait which will help to introduce them as personalities. If, in addition, Thomas can have worked through scenes in which Sir Anthony discovered the approaching fit of the gout and rushed Julia and Harry and Mr Kate and the postilion to Bath within the hour's warning, Thomas will have captured something of the excitement of his part of the situation. Fag, on the other hand, can work with Captain Absolute, assisting him in his wooing of Lydia, and his change of personalities into Ensign Beverly, and he can get to know this "lady of very singular taste" as he moves about Bath, enjoying its entertainments. Fag and Thomas also need to build up in improvisation this relationship of men of a similar class, who enjoy talking about the people for whom they work and are anxious to share with each other a good thing when they come on to it. By the time they come on to playing this first scene in its full sequence they would have appreciated sharing a bit of news, a bit of gossip, a bit of fashion and an exchange of where the best entertainment is to be found.

So it is in most of these reported situations that we aim to bring the scene for the actors out of the dead area of dull reportage into a lively exchange of happenings between human beings who have something to say because it matters to them.

CHAPTER 20

Reality Outside the Text

Within the text, as we have seen, the author very often explicitly presents a detailed description of what takes place or has taken place outside our area of vision. However, at other times he leaves a good deal to actor and producer, while he only implies the life beyond the play. Once we understand the nature of a dramatic text we can recognize these hints which occur throughout and create for ourselves in rehearsals the reality "off-stage".

In some plays the hints are obvious enough, but even these need to be felt physically and experienced to help the actors to comprehend the situation fully. The Malayan jungle world outside "the deserted store hut" in Willis Hall's *The Long and the Short and the Tall* is given a brief mention in the opening description: there are short bursts of gunfire at the beginning and again at the end, and Mitchem and Johnstone tell us a little of their expedition, but the whole world of Malayan jungle warfare, of the possibility of meeting a Japanese contingent and so on, can be more vividly realized if we play some of this through in improvised form. The marching with heavy kit and ammunition through difficult country and constant danger cannot be adequately grasped by reading or talk, or even seeing a film, and the more that this can be discovered with the body the more we can live the full life of the play. This kind of improvisation would also give the actors an opportunity of discovering the effect that climate and conditions have upon relationships.

The same sort of need is seen in plays like Wesker's *Chips With Everything*, where the whole of the Air Force life is exemplified only, and more experience is required if the acting is to show that dimension which the script demands. For Smiler's full reaction throughout his desertion scene and afterwards he needs to feel this building out of the physical confinement and the constant drill of foot and mind throughout his training. Pip, too, needs more experience than can possibly come out of rehearsing solely on the text, and the conscripts and the officers can play out their relationships with greater conviction and understanding if they have the opportunity of working on other routine matters linked with the Air Force life.

Many plays presented at the Theatre Royal, Stratford East, enjoyed this kind of treatment, and actors found great benefit from, for instance, working for long periods in vigorously confined areas in preparation for Brendan Behan's *The Quare Fellow* (see pp. 4-5), and were enabled to have greater insight into the situation through these improvisations. Similarly, when working on Shelagh Delaney's *A Taste of Honey*, to drag imaginary cases and trunks along gloomy corridors and up difficult staircases and into unfriendly rooms considerably helped the feeling of being constantly on the move and having to live in particularly comfortless spaces.

All this preparation for the actor enables him to make the playing out in performance of the situation have a quality which gives to the audience added insight into the text, not just on an intellectual plane, but on a physical and emotional one as well. We seem to take it for granted that a dancer needs regular physical training in order that his body should be kept supple and responsive for the moment of performance, but we seem less willing to realize that the actor needs physical, mental and emotional fitness. We accept that he needs training in the first instance (though there are some who doubt this), but we are less inclined to regard it as worth while that he should work around the text in the process of rehearsals. In fact, it seems to us that just as the dancer will spend some time in physical warming-up immediately before each performance, so the actor would benefit from a period of physical, imaginative and vocal warming-up before each of his performances. It would not be at all difficult for him to spend about twenty minutes in preparing for, say, the prison atmosphere of *The Quare Fellow*, or the jungle suspense of *The Long and the Short and the Tall*, and, in fact, when this has been tried actors have found that they could go easily and directly from the improvised trek through the jungle into the hut where the performance was given. Similarly, a play like Edward Albee's *Who's Afraid of Virginia Woolf?* can be played with added understanding if the Faculty party in which Martha invites Honey and Nick over is played out, prior to each performance. This can help both George and Martha particularly to build the pace and fire of their dialogue, so that when they come in at the outset they do not have to begin cold.

The first phase of Act 3 of *The Crucible* takes place off-stage and is the voices of Giles and Martha Corey raised against their accusers. For this to find its true life and pace, an enactment of the trial of Martha will establish the excitement, and enable the flow into the vestry room to be carried out in the appropriate rhythm. Judge Hawthorne's entry, followed by Danforth, can then be worked on, experimenting so that the change of atmosphere and pace brings out the build to the entry of Mary Warren and Proctor. So we could work on the scene phase by phase until it builds naturally through the moments of rising hysteria to Proctor's denunciation of Danforth and Hale's exit, with, "I denounce these proceedings; I quit this court."

Perhaps future theatre design could even begin to consider actors' needs and allow some space where an actor could prepare himself imaginatively before "making an entrance". Although for the most part totally inadequate, dressing-rooms are provided where an actor is given some space and facilities for donning his costume. Everybody recognizes, too, the need for time to be spent on make-up, and we accept as commonplace that this art is often elaborate and must be carried out before every performance. It seems odd that we should recognize the need for building-up external manifestations of character in costume and make-up before each performance, but somehow seem to regard the internal building-up as that which has been carried out once and for all in earlier work on the text. In places, the idea of using make-up is being discontinued as more actors are called upon to play characters like themselves, but surely it is reasonable that the half-hour before each show in which the actor's presence is required in the theatre should be spent with his fellow actors in keeping his whole artistry fit.

The same demand is also necessary every time the actor leaves the stage. In some cases, of course, there will be no more than time to make a hurried change of costume or rush to another part of the stage in time for the next entrance, but in any case the greatest need is that imaginative preparation should have been carried through in rehearsals. When Jimmy Porter in *Look Back in Anger* leaves the stage to play his trumpet, though he may not, in fact, play it, it will help him in understanding the character and his emotional drive if he has handled a trumpet in rehearsals and been able to realize something of what Jimmy gained from his musical expression beyond the confined attic space that he shared with Alison. Similarly, Cliff should know his room, so that he leaves the Porters to move into a different atmosphere, and can stand in contrast to Jimmy when they are both with Alison. Even if there is no opportunity to do much more than the briefest imaginative recollection after an exit, and before an entrance, this, together with the preliminary preparation before the play, will give the acting a continuity and impact which would otherwise be almost impossible to sustain.

In some plays the imaginary time lapse between one exit and the next entrance may be considerable. Age and experience may well only be hinted at in the text and it is up to the actor to bring this into the realms of understanding. In Shakespeare's *The Winter's Tale*, for instance, we jump over sixteen years with just a chorus, so that it is most important that Leontes should have some physical and imaginative understanding of what this would have meant to him. Hermione leaves us early in the play and does not reappear until we see her statue come to life towards the very end. Even in a situation like this, where there is a good deal of romantic and fairy-tale quality, improvisation which leads to an understanding of what lies behind these jumps of circumstance can aid the actor and reinforce the experience for the audience. An attempt at understanding Hermione's feelings at being kept away from Leontes and the world for sixteen years allows the actress to be able to build on her comprehension of the relationship and devotion she has with her husband, and when this is linked with other explorations into the kind of play with which we are dealing, we can ensure that we shall not be presented with any glib fairy tale, but that the play can retain the richness of myth and legend.

The approach we are suggesting is really aimed at striking a blow at the "let's click into it" school of acting. If acting is associated with living, and the living is to go on at any particular depth, we cannot accept the switching on and off. Most of our feelings and attitudes build comparatively slowly and the technique the actor aims to acquire should be the sure control of this building. The technique he very often acquires is that he can "turn on" the surface response associated with feeling, which makes for a completely different response in the audience who, similarly, accept a surface experience. What we must do is to be able to distinguish between the surface and the depth approach. Obviously we do not want the same approach to acting in revue as in tragedy. The vital thing is that we should not accept one for the other, and that we should expect to have to make a different contribution and a different response with each dramatic occasion.

CHAPTER 21

Establishing the Language and Imagery

In all the work so far we have been exploring the text and discovering what lies within and around the words the author has given us. By this stage we will know a considerable amount of the text and will find ourselves using it. It may well be that because there has been no tension built around the need to learn the words already the script is known more accurately and fully than under a system which asks for lines learned first. It is not uncommon for a producer who has made no effort to learn the words of a text to be able to prompt his actors who presumably have been making every effort. Actors, too, find that it is sometimes easier to remember another person's part than to remember their own, both of which incidents suggest that the memory works more responsively without tension.

The language which the author has given us is a combination of meaning, rhythm and vocabulary. So far, our concern has been directed particularly to meaning and rhythm, so we are now going to concentrate on the vocabulary.

The Greeks in the great fifth century B.C. had already realized interrelationship in movement, rhythm and words as the chorus beat out a pattern with feet and body which reinforced the words they chanted. This is a particularly useful way of making our bodies and minds respond to the ideas presented.

First take the broad pattern of the images which affect the language used throughout the play. Symbols occur strongly in the work of many dramatists, and to grasp the impact of these is a sound basis for understanding, and therefore remembering, the language. Ibsen often employed symbols consciously, underlining their function. In *The Lady from the Sea* we might explore in movement terms the sea theme, working with the groups on patterns illustrating the power of the waves, shipwrecks, mermaids, storms, mists, the mystery of the moon and tide relationship, and so on. Even a short session of this kind can make the language patterns evident and meaning clearer.

A similar thing might be followed through with *The Wild Duck*, taking wildness and captivity, freedom and restriction, as our main line of exploration. We can also be on the look-out for the playwright's more subconscious use of the symbol and discover its even greater significance in the plays perhaps. In *Hedda Gabler*, for instance, we can work on the theme of fire, pursuing it as a destructive force, as shown by Hedda's burning of the manuscript, but also following it through as an energy force, seen in Tesman, Lovborg and Hedda herself. We can notice the moments when it is burning with greatest vigour, times when its flames are frustrated, and moments when it is scarcely a flicker. In fact, each of the characters in the play can be followed as a fire, and each with his or her relationship to the literal fire in the Tesmans' stove. In *An Enemy of the People* the symbolism is drawn from the soil; so in these four plays it is interesting to note how Ibsen has taken the elements earth, air, fire and water and used them as his frame of reference, and all are particularly good for exploration in improvised movement terms.

Other playwrights will make a different use of symbol, but wherever it occurs insight into the playwright's language and awareness of it can be achieved through this movement approach.

Similarly, when a writer uses a recurrent image or image-sequence, we can dance out the words and some of their associations. The strong symbolism in *King Lear* is provided by the blinding of Gloucester, whose condition reinforces the spiritual sightlessness of Lear, but apart from this we can work in movement terms on the recurrent images of nature, sensing the ever-present emphasis upon its more loathsome manifestations. We might also make ourselves aware of the repetition of "Nothing", placed beside man's desire for everything. In spite of the impressive studies by Caroline Spurgeon and Wilson Knight, it is still possible for groups to make their own discoveries sometimes quite fresh, from the texts. Most people see the belly and body imagery in *Coriolanus*, but not much is said about the bird and beast images which keep appearing throughout the play. Once a group is aware of such verbal themes, meaning becomes clearer, the language more significant, and the words remain in the memory.

Many other Elizabethan and Jacobean dramatists are rewarding for being delved into in this way, but a similar approach can be taken with modern authors like Beckett, for instance. If we follow through the references in *Godot* to religion, sacrifice and redemption, we can again grasp something further of the pattern and come nearer to the language structure.

As previously, the approach has been from the overall pattern of the play to the specific detail. Groups might be reminded here of their discoveries of the rhythm of speech and style of language and apply similar principles to some of the more difficult speeches in the play on which they are working. In emphasizing the speeches as expressions of shaped thought the tape recorder can be of particular value. Supposing we get the actor playing Hamlet to record his speech beginning, "Oh, what a rogue and peasant slave am I", reading it from the text, and expressing it in a manner which he believes will bring out the thought and mood. We can in rehearsal get him to move to the play-back of his own voice in such a way as to express in movement the detail of the language. Then he might take certain portions of the speech and work on them in greater detail from the movement point of view. There is no need for him to attempt to dumb-show explanation of the words; all he is aiming to do is to bring each phrase and image into the conscious part of his mind so that at one and the same time he is grasping the exact turn of the language and what lies behind it. As a kind of synthesis then, he can sit and think the speech through as his words come from the tape recorder.

Or, taking Titania's speech in *A Midsummer Night's Dream*, beginning "These are the forgeries of jealousy", Titania can either move through a movement sequence to her tape-recorded speaking of the passage or, as she speaks it aloud, she can watch her attendants work on a movement pattern which reinforces the words she is saying. This is not a performance, and is aimed only to make the words themselves gain more life and significance. Phrases like:

> By paved fountain, or by rushy brook,
> Or in the beached margent of the sea,

might readily suggest movement sequences, but "the forgeries of jealousy" will demand more thought and exploration. Then, once the obvious and ham meanings have been overcome, more subtle and perceptive means will suggest themselves. What is happening is that the players are having to think into the images, put them on to a sensual plane and so give them an added dimension. Finally, when Titania returns to speaking this speech in its context the words are more likely to retain an alive quality and so come over to the listeners with heightened understanding.

Words are symbols, so even in works of complete prose texts we can follow a similar method. A good deal of fun can be enjoyed in comedy. The comedians in the two-act version of N. F. Simpson's *A Resounding Tinkle* have a great many words to put over, and some of the comedy is inherent in the visual aspect of the words. When the first comedian is being the doctor, and examining the second comedian, who is explaining his ailments, the dialogue tends to take a natural shape once the sequence of events has been grasped. But later, when they are arguing about what can be expected of an audience and enjoying their "flying off at a tangent", closer observation of the "stream of consciousness" is needed:

> As for problems, of course a horse on the stage presents problems. Of course it does. And suppose we solve all the problems it presents? What happens? We end up with more problems than we started with. Because that's the way problems propagate their species. A problem left to itself dries up or goes rotten. But fertilize a problem with a solution – you'll hatch out dozens. It's better than breeding budgerigars. There isn't anything very challenging about a budgerigar. There's a limit to what you can do by way of experiment.

Improvised work on such a section, both in movement and words, can be devised to bring out both meaning and comedy. In just the sentence, for instance, "Fertilise a problem with a solution – you'll hatch out dozens", the actors will find much amusement in a laboratory for incubating premature problems, and at the same time will be gaining insight into the ways in which the minds of these characters work. Such a speech is clearly so full of comic possibilities that the actors need this time to ponder over the images, so that the speech can have something of its full humorous impact in performance.

In all plays there is the need for this constant bringing of the language from the cold world on the page to the realized thought in the mind, so that even while we are emphasizing the importance of using the actual words in the text we are thinking of them as symbols conveying meaning. More mundane works can be approached with constant questions by the group leader or producer, so that while the words are having this measure of concentration they are still thought of as a means of communication. Instead of a producer asking for a particular inflexion here, a pause there, or emphasis at some other point, he can ask, "What do you want me to understand by that?" This will probably lead to an explanation in words other than those of the author, but eventually the producer can ask that the actor returns to the text, speaking it in a manner which will enable the desired meaning to be conveyed. This may well result in a change of inflexion, an alteration in the rate, or in a pause, but it will mean that this has arisen out of the speech and the actor's understanding of it, rather than something he takes on mechanically from elsewhere.

Longer paraphrase and alternation of text and own word interpretations will also aid in a grasp of the words and as it comes to final stages groups can work with a tape recorder, using the text at times and at other times working without the text in an effort to present a radio version of the drama. This approach, it seems to us, is much to be preferred to what some actors refer to as a "word rehearsal", which means a gabble-through the lines in a routine manner. If the language of the text is of any value at all, it is surely worth intelligent understanding and expression at all times.

CHAPTER 22

Relating the Visual to the Text

During .the ensuing conversation, Mrs Elton turns the easy
chair back to its original position, shuts the bottom half of the
window and partly closes the top half. She then puts the window
table into position underneath the window and sets the two
dining chairs tidily above and below the window table. Finally
she opens the curtains of the upstage window.

It would seem that in following through Mrs Elton's "business"
in this stage direction from an acting edition of *The Deep Blue Sea*
by Terence Rattigan we are not expected to reason why. These
actions may be said to add interest or variety throughout the conversation, but they certainly cannot be held to be pointing, or
illuminating, the exchange between Hester and Mrs Elton. The
trouble is that acting editions are now being prepared for all kinds
of plays, from Shakespeare to Simpson (the Greeks are probably
next for treatment), and when the majority of people get hold of
these they feel that these instructions are imperative, and that
somehow the details of the vast staircase, French windows, and
collection of antique furniture are vital to the presentation of the
play.

What a person does on stage is part of his character, his mood
and his relationship both with people and things. What he finds on
stage in the way of furniture or properties should be that which is
necessary for the action of the play or the creation of character, or
the creation of atmosphere. A play does require movement, but
how much should be determined by our knowledge of the play and
not by our knowledge of the stage directions. The overall concept
of the production is something which must arise from the producer's study of the play, and the group's exploration of it. What
entrances does this play demand? Where should they be placed to
great advantage in view of what we understand of the writing?
This means that the actors themselves understand not that the
door is "left centre", and the staircase "down right", say, but why
they are there, and what contribution they will make to the play

by being in just those positions. In the same way, instead of having to try to remember that on a particular line the actor gets up and goes over to the table, he feels this necessity from his understanding of the play and the character. Similarly, a character must see the point of being close to another character or separated from him, and not feel that this is dictated arbitrarily by the edition or the producer.

It is still possible for a producer who wishes to work in detail on a text before meeting his company to have a clear visual conception of the play and to arrive at early rehearsals with an overall pattern of movement in his mind. If what he has planned of movement and grouping has any relationship to the text and the needs of the play, he will be able to approach his concept very nearly by drawing responses from the actors. Such questions as, "What are you saying? Does it suggest any physical reaction to you? Can you find any way of making that clear on a visual level?" will help him to draw out the response for which he is looking. It may so happen that, because the actor is a different person from the producer, he comes upon a different solution to the problem posed. It is then up to the producer, or the group watching, to decide whether this is desirable in the circumstances or whether the actor should be asked to look for a further possible way of resolving the question. If a producer can keep an open mind, he can very often use to good effect the natural responses of the actor and quite often when actors have developed a good sense of grouping the visual impact of a scene can flow naturally, reinforcing the text to great effect. With inexperienced actors, or those who have learned tricks over the years by a different approach to the acting situation, it may well be necessary to reverse the process. The producer may have to ask, "Why are you crossing over there? Or sitting down? Or using that gesture?" Placed in a position like this, the actor may well be able to find an excuse and, again, it must be up to the producer to decide whether this is justifiable and whether it helps with the overall interpretation of the play.

If we are thinking specifically, say, of Anouilh's version of the St Joan story in his play *The Lark*, we are not hindered by many directions, since all that he asks for is "a simple, neutral setting". We have, however, to ask what the play needs in the way of visual appeal, and consider what will contribute to the most effective communication of it. Early work will enable the groups to realize

that the author's approach is one in which he uses the trial of Joan
as the centre of our attention, and during this we are given a
number of flashbacks to the more significant moments of her
career. There are, in fact, two distinct levels of playing: the concrete and more permanent court of the present and the more
imaginative recollections of the past. This helps us in the approach
to the setting, for if we can present two physical levels this will be
underlining the approach of the text. The levels might be presented
in several ways, but the feeling we derive from the text is that the
trial is surrounding Joan. The incidents of her life are recalled
within the court, and this, too, can be given visual presentation in
the play. Similarly, it will be noticed that there is a certain sequence
in these recollected incidents: Joan begins in prison and throughout the play we go on a kind of conducted tour through her life.
This may also be used in our visual approach, if each of these
imagined recalls can be presented in different parts of the acting
area in such a way as to represent the time sequence. Such obser-
vations will contribute to the planning of the production and would
probably have been made as the result of improvised work on the
play as a whole. Once the specific playing areas have been decided
upon, the detailed work can begin.

The characters in the trial itself: Cauchon, the Promoter, the
Inquisitor, Ladvenu, are likely to be clearest placed on the upper
level looking down upon Joan. Certain movements of the play will
suggest a closer contact – for instance, Cauchon's long pleading
with Joan just before her submission, will be felt by the actors in
their improvisations to demand a closer physical relationship.

Every movement pattern, in fact, can be seen as that which
supports visually the mood, pace and temperature of the text.
When Joan (in flashback) is being beaten and ill-treated by her
father for the "lies" about her voices, a fair amount of movement
is indicated by the nature of the scene. His threatening tones and
forceful action suggest that he cannot be still and that Joan is likely
to be backing away:

FATHER: What are you doing here, eh? Tell me what you're
    waiting about here for, when you know you ought to be
    indoors, eating your supper!
JOAN: I didn't know it was so late. I had lost count of the time.

Give opportunities for work in pairs, where an angry father

scolds his wayward daughter, building up to his sheer exasperation at her "outrageous" protests of innocence, and a movement pattern will emerge. It is then up to the leader to select and, working with the actors, shape the best pattern for the play and the overall development of it in production. Follow this by improvisations on the contrasting scene between Joan and her mother. Here, the mother is comforting the daughter and taking her side against the father. Working on similar scenes, actors will soon make it clear that very little movement is necessary and that the scene is visually aided by a stillness which comes as an emphasizing contrast after the movement and pace of the previous scene. Encourage actors to be on the look-out for movement indications suggested by changes of tone or thought. After a speech of maternal comforting, Joan protests:

> It isn't marriage that I have to think of, mother. The blessed St Michael has told me I should leave the village, put on a man's clothes, and go and find his highness the Dauphin, to save the realm of France.

In the previous speech Joan's mother was "rocking her in her arms", but after this she replies –

> (*severely*): Joan, I speak nicely and gently to you, but I won't have you talking wickedness.

This alteration of attitude might well call for an alteration of position which, in its turn, visually emphasizes the change of tone. In the previous speech, mother was holding her daughter to comfort her, and now she is being severe – some changed position is needed. This the actors will undoubtedly sense once they have felt the emotional and relationship pattern. A further important point to notice is that the movement change of Joan's mother does not come where it is mechanically indicated on the page of the text: "MOTHER (*severely*)", but begins earlier, in Joan's speech, when she tells her mother that she has to leave the village and put on man's clothes. So, improvised work, besides helping the discovery of what movement is necessary, also aids actors to realize when it should occur, and how it is carried out.

The fact that we are thinking about the way in which the visual can aid communication of other aspects of the text indicates that we are thinking in terms of the participation of an audience. There-fore, every time groups show their work to others in rehearsals, they are helping to ensure that communication is carried out with clarity. There need be no adherence to worn-out or clichéd tech-niques if our standards remain associated with questions like, "Does the movement aid understanding?" and, "Is the under-standing communicated with clarity?"

In some plays very little movement is called for. Samuel Beckett, for instance, in plays like *Happy Days* or *Endgame*, or most notably *Play*, cuts movement to a minimum, while other plays, like Henry Livings's *Nil Carborundum*, call for a great deal. All the visual impact of a play must be motivated by the author's words and his aim as understood by actor and producer. In a play like *Philip Hotz's Fury* by Max Frisch, the author is clear about the move-ments in the dialogue for the entrances and exits of the characters, but the timing of, for example, the removal men with their sawn-down furniture or buckets of rubbish is something which it is essential for the actors themselves to feel. Their presence and action make a visual contribution to the play and must rise from the three-dimensional demands of the text. Where and how they enter, where the furniture or debris is placed is something which the group can explore through improvisation.

During the earlier sessions, which have been designed to explore the text, all kinds of interesting and effective groupings and movement patterns will have emerged. The producer or leader can have kept notes of these and can now work on recapturing the best moments. The great advantage is that these are natural responses of the actors in the situation and are therefore likely to be working in harmony with the text and without any overconsciousness of the "theatrical" situation.

With the increasing emphasis that is being placed these days on the open stage, scenery is becoming more and more three dimensional, so that movement within it tends to call for an imaginative response to this stage architecture, instead of it being something in front of which the action is being played. At other times, of course, there is very little scenery used and the movement of the actors, together with the odd symbolic effect, is emphasized. In Shaffer's *The Royal Hunt of the Sun*, at Chichester Festival Theatre, the Spanish expeditionary party in South America climb parts of the Andes. No scenery whatever is employed, and everything is most effectively suggested by the actors' movement and mime. By the same means, the terrible bloodshed and slaughter of the South American Indians by the Spaniards is suggested and the whole of the movement pattern reinforced by the effective use of a vast stained cloth which is drawn like a stream of blood from the centre of the back of the acting area, eventually covering the entire space, giving the impression of a blood-washed battlefield after terrifying slaughter. How much of this actually came from improvisation we do not know, but it seems likely that the basic idea of the battle was explored through improvisation, and the final effects fixed as the result of group work.

Several of the writers whose work is coming to be known as the "theatre of the absurd" have a keen sense of the visual, and an understanding that, while what we see can support what we hear, at times it is more effective to leave the visual effect to make its own impact. This is, in fact, what Ionesco does in some of his plays, notably *The New Tenant*, where most of the gripping claustrophobia is achieved by what we see. Ionesco's directions are clear, though he still leaves opportunity for group work and individual feeling to play its part in the creation of the scene. The whole of the enclosing of the new tenant in his room packed by his furniture and belongings is a combination of visual rhythm interspersed by verbal rhythm, building to the final moment when the light is switched off.

There are moments in Beckett's work when he, like Ionesco at times, makes use of the opposition of the visual and the aural. Often, what Vladimir and Estragon say is in contradiction to what they do, so heightening the zany effect and our sense of futility.

ESTRAGON : I'm going. (*He does not move*)

VLADIMIR : And yet . . . (*Pause*) . . . how is it – this is not boring you, I hope – how is it that of the four evangelists only one speaks of a thief being saved? The four of them were there – or thereabouts, and only one speaks of a thief being saved. (*Pause.*) Come on, Gogo, return the ball, can't you, once in a way?

ESTRAGON (*with exaggerated enthusiasm*): I find this really most extraordinarily interesting.

Here the visual is still playing its part, but stillness creates the impact rather than action.

Because drama makes a demand upon the actor as a whole person and the audience as a total being, every one of the aspects of the play which we have considered will have its visual aspect. The mood, the rhythm, the characters, the narrative element, the language and the shape of the play as a whole will all be seen as well as heard and felt, not as separate entities, but as items integrated into the moment of enactment. Perhaps the best test of the visual effect is that it draws attention to the author's aim, rather than being any attempt to make up for what we consider to be his deficiencies.

CHAPTER 23

Planning a Rehearsal Programme

We have tried so far to bear in mind the various needs of those approaching the texts from different points of emphasis. Some may be thinking of recreational work, or of a text for an examination, some may be using a text for more educational exploration of human relationships, while others will be working towards directing the play in performance.

For those who are thinking of play production primarily, there is a need clearly, amidst all the free exploration of thoughts and feelings derived from the script, for a definite development towards a first-night date. As we saw when improvising without using a text, we require some sense of direction and each session on the text should be aimed towards a deepening of understanding so that all rehearsals build in some way on the work that has gone before.

Even before rehearsals begin the producer has to spend a considerable number of hours reading the play, thinking about it and researching into its background, but he need not necessarily use his knowledge to overinfluence his company or prevent them from making their own discoveries. His task is rather to employ his understanding in such a way as to help his actors to be able to find the life of the text for themselves. Planned rehearsals might be organized in three phases:

1. Exploration and interpretation
2. Excavation and evocation
3. Co-ordination and consolidation.

Time spent on rehearsals varies with almost every company. Some find themselves still working on a one-week repertory while there are other companies who can enjoy a six- or eight-week rehearsal programme. So far in this country we have not experienced the breadth of a six month or one year exploration of a play. When a play is kept in repertory like those at Stratford or the National Theatre, clearly an excellent opportunity occurs for further progress in understanding and projecting this understanding in performance. Too often, however, performances after a while suggest deterioration in quality and playing seems to lose spontaneity.

With non-professional groups conditions are equally varying. Most give considerably less time to rehearsals than the professional groups, although they must clearly require more. Very few companies of either professionals or amateurs consider having regular studio groups where members can keep in touch with the general imaginative practice involved in the art of acting. In arranging rehearsals all could programme for the inclusion of sessions in which the main aim was the development of the actor and not just the presentation of the play.

Each section of the rehearsal time will have its own shape and direction ·

I. EXPLORATION AND INTERPRETATION

The director might first choose to introduce the company to the theme of the play through movement or improvisations devised to bring out topical equivalents of the implications within the play, or he may give imaginative exercises aimed at raising questions about aspects of the play and its background. He might then move on to (or he could decide to start with) improvisations for discovering the unity of the play, aiming to ensure that his company at this stage becomes familiar with the sequence and phases of the play. If actors can become familiar with relationships between one part of the action and another, later working establishing shape and rhythm will prove much easier. In aiding acquaintance with the play the director can arrange for every actor to play as many parts as possible. Most of us feel that rehearsal time is never long enough, so it is especially important that we do not waste any of it. We need to learn how to organize it so that everyone is working all the time. A great deal, especially in this early part of rehearsal, can be discovered by the actors working with each other and the director arranging the overall scheme. At given points actors might look at each other's work and derive benefit from noticing other approaches and points of view. Quite often concentrated work over a few hours at a stretch is more useful than more diffused working over a great many hours. The vital thing is to have a definite objective for each session within the programme and to focus all attention towards it. Once a clear understanding of the shape is being grasped, the style of the piece will begin to be apparent and further improvisations on this can be given. Towards the end of the first third of the rehearsals everyone should be aware of the main elements and the unity of the play. The director with his group can then decide upon the particular approach to be taken and any points of disagreement in interpretation can be put to an acting test of what feels and looks most appropriate for the context in which the presentation is being given.

Casting

At this point the director and company are in a good position to be able to decide which players are best able to cope with various parts. In practice, when casting comes at the end of a period of exploration some quite exciting results are apparent. Instead of apportioning the parts before or after a cursory reading, or as a result of past experiences of what an actor has played well (or *not* played well), a decision can be reached on what the actor has done with a part in association with his fellow actors and in the complete acting situation demanded by this particular play.

2. EXCAVATION AND EVOCATION

This second phase of the work involves a deepening of the understanding and more specific work on characterization, atmosphere, detailed interpretation and overall bringing the text to life. Actors should find themselves regularly searching the text for answers to questions raised in improvisations, and time not involved in working with other actors would be spent individually in reading and becoming more familiar with the character's thoughts and his exact words given by the author.

Together the group work on relationships and seeing how these are affected by and affect the movement and the grouping. There will be special work on the scene by scene atmosphere and care will be taken to ensure that all parts of the play receive adequate work. Some system is necessary. Rehearsals at this stage might be arranged on a chronological approach or it might be one which involves contrasts and similarities of mood, or scenes may be rehearsed together which involve similar characters. It may well be that some section of the play will receive more attention than others (according to the difficulty), but in any case the director will endeavour to keep his group in touch with all sections of the play and their relationship one with another.

It is during this section of rehearsals that the director will fix a date by which actors will be expected to know and use the text accurately. Throughout, rehearsal of the play can take place with copies of the text of the play at the side of the playing area for reference. All the acting can be done without texts in hands to hinder and restrict the players. As time goes on they will find themselves coming closer and closer to a thorough knowledge of the author's words. The first necessity for any actor is to find out why he says what is there in the text and then to understand the thought sequence.

Texts held in the hand, however skilfully, always restrict the actor in rehearsals; they hinder easy movement and when being read prevent eye contact between members of the group. There is a tendency under these conditions to be so preoccupied with the script and so concerned with keeping the place and coming in on cue that it becomes almost impossible for actors to concern themselves with the real business of imagining, listening, responding and feeling. Script-held rehearsals too easily grow mechanical. There must, however, be no mistake – the actors work considerably with the script, but the approach is different. Instead of trying to learn it rote fashion, they spend the time on the script reading it, pondering it and understanding not just the words of their own character but their speeches in context and as part of the whole play. Once we really understand anything there is very little effort required in remembering it.

3. CO-ORDINATION AND CONSOLIDATION

The final third of rehearsal time is one of bringing together work done in previous sessions. The clarity of visual pattern, overall pace and climaxes are established. Here more attention is paid to continuity and flow of the play, so that actors can develop their work in the sequence in which they will eventually perform it to an audience. In first rehearsals in this period it may be better to work on the flow of the action in sections, and as time proceeds progress to the overall sustained flow. At least once a week there should be a complete run through the play with as few interruptions as possible. There should be no mechanical prompting, as this tends to bring only a mechanical response from the actors. If actors realize at the outset that there will be no prompter, none is ever needed. When a difficulty or loss of concentration arises other characters can help out, retaining the mood and the shape of the scene. In this way the actor who has been momentarily lost returns to the sequence easily through his overall knowledge of the play.

The kind of play being worked upon will determine the variety of aims and approaches in these complete run-throughs. If it is a costume play, the actors would do well to have worked all along with at least tokens of clothing which help them in character creation and mood, and if the final costumes are available early, these should be worn. In any case it is important for props and furniture to be used in rehearsal sessions so that the actors can feel these in relation to their part and develop the right use and attitude towards them. Final rehearsals will then be much more directed towards sustaining continuity of mood and character than towards coping with props or the novelty of putting on costume.

The earlier all the more technical aspects of production can be brought into the play the better. This will enable lighting, sound, setting and so on to have time to become well integrated. Whenever possible members of the stage-management staff will have taken part in early improvisations, and so they will have come to an understanding of the needs of the play. The more we can do to help all to realize that they are part of a group co-operating on every aspect of production, the more we are likely to find the technical side built into the rhythm and flow, carried out with insight and understanding and not just isolated departments supplying the trimmings.

One of the aims of the director will always be to retain a relaxed atmosphere amongst the company. This does not mean that there will be a sloppy approach. Work is being done, but without unnecessary tension which would only hinder the free flow of imagination and concentration. The director will also try to ensure that the approach retains the vital quality of spontaneity. Whenever he feels undue tension or over-relaxation it will be his task to devise ways to bring the necessary change about. If things become nervous and overanxious he might break this by asking his company to spend part of a rehearsal period acting the play in another style – say comic opera or mock Italian or by changing parts so that the women play the men's roles and the men the women's. He will also continue devising improvisations around the text and the characters so that fresh thoughts are always keeping the situation alive.

If at most rehearsals one group working has been watched by another group, so that they could learn from each other, actors are developing concentration and fringe awareness all along. It is good, then, to increase the number of people participating as audience in the last stages of rehearsals and to build this to an appropriate number by the time we reach our last two or three dress-rehearsals. So, when the first night arrives there is no obvious break or feeling of theatricality: the process has been one of transition in which the actors' discovery of the play and their treatment of its living interpretation has developed to moments in time when its continuous presentation is shared with an audience. The creative process might well go on with each performance, making the drama sustain its freshness and spontaneity, benefiting both actor and audience.

GENERAL INDEX

OTHER GROVE PRESS DRAMA AND THEATER PAPERBACKS

E487   ABE, KOBO / Friends / $2.45

B415   ARDEN, JOHN / John Arden Plays: One (Serjeant Musgrave's Dance, The Workhouse Donkey, Armstrong's Last Goodnight) / $3.95

B109   ARDEN, JOHN / Three Plays (Live Like Pigs, The Waters of Babylon, The Happy Haven) / $2.45

E610   ARRABAL, FERNANDO / And They Put Handcuffs on the Flowers / $1.95

E611   ARRABAL, FERNANDO / Garden of Delights / $2.95

E521   ARRABAL, FERNANDO / Guernica and Other Plays (The Labyrinth, The Tricycle, Picnic on the Battlefield) / $4.95

E532   ARTAUD, ANTONIN / The Cenci / $3.95

E425   BARAKA, IMAMU AMIRI (LeRoi Jones) / The Baptism and The Toilet: Two Plays / $2.45 [See also Grove Press Modern Drama, John Lahr, ed., E633 / $5.95]

E670   BARAKA, IMAMU AMIRI (LeRoi Jones) / The System of Dante's Hell, The Dead Lecturer and Tales / $4.95

E471   BECKETT, SAMUEL / Cascando and Other Short Dramatic Pieces (Words and Music, Eh Joe, Play, Come and Go, Film) / $3.95

        BECKETT, SAMUEL / The Collected Works of Samuel Beckett in Twenty-two Volumes / $85.00

E96   BECKETT, SAMUEL / Endgame / $1.95

E318   BECKETT, SAMUEL / Happy Days / $2.45

E692   BECKETT, SAMUEL / I Can't Go On; I'll Go On / $6.95

E33   BECKETT, SAMUEL / Waiting for Godot / $1.95 [See also Seven Plays of the Modern Theater, Harold Clurman, ed., E 717 / $6.95]

B411   BEHAN, BRENDAN / The Complete Plays (The Hostage, The Quare Fellow, Richard's Cork Leg, Three One Act Plays for Radio) / $3.95

B79   BEHAN, BRENDAN / The Quare Fellow and The Hostage: Two Plays / $2.95 [See also Seven Plays of the Modern Theater, Harold Clurman, ed., E717 / $6.95]

E90   BETTI, UGO / Three Plays (The Queen and the Rebels, The Burnt Flower-Bed, Summertime) / $3.95

B120   BRECHT, BERTOLT / Galileo / $1.95 [See also Seven Plays by Bertolt Brecht, GP248 / $12.50]

B117   BRECHT, BERTOLT / The Good Woman of Setzuan / $1.95 [See also Seven Plays by Bertolt Brecht, GP248 / $12.50]

B80   BRECHT, BERTOLT / The Jewish Wife and Other Short Plays (In Search of Justice, The Informer, The Elephant Calf, The Measures Taken, The Exception and the Rule, Salzburg Dance of Death) / $1.95

B414   BRECHT, BERTOLT / The Mother / $2.95

GP248 BRECHT, BERTOLT / Seven Plays by Bertolt Brecht (In the Swamp, A Man's A Man, Saint Joan of the Stockyards, Mother Courage and Her Children, Galileo, The Good Woman of Setzuan, The Caucasian Chalk Circle) / $12.50

B333   BRECHT, BERTOLT / The Threepenny Opera / $1.95

B193   BULGAKOV, MIKHAIL / Heart of a Dog / $2.95

B147   BULGAKOV, MIKHAIL / The Master and Margarita / $3.95

E693   CHEKHOV, ANTON / The Cherry Orchard / $2.95

E717   CLURMAN, HAROLD, ed. / Seven Plays of the Modern Theater (Waiting for Godot by Samuel Beckett, The Quare Fellow by Brendan Behan, A Taste of Honey by Shelagh Delaney, The Connection by Jack Gelber, The Balcony by Jean Genet, Rhinoceros by Eugene Ionesco, The Birthday Party by Harold Pinter) / $6.95

E159   DELANEY, SHELAGH / A Taste of Honey / $2.95 [See also Seven Plays of the Modern Theater, Harold Clurman, ed., E717 / $6.95]

E380   DURRENMATT, FRIEDRICH / The Physicists / $2.95

E344   DURRENMATT, FRIEDRICH / The Visit / $2.95

B132   GARSON, BARBARA / MacBird! /$1.95

E223   GELBER, JACK / The Connection / $3.95 [See also Seven Plays of the Modern Theater, Harold Clurman, ed., E717 / $6.95]

E130   GENET, JEAN / The Balcony / $2.95 [See also Seven Plays of the Modern Theater, Harold Clurman, ed., E717 / $6.95]

E208   GENET, JEAN / The Blacks: A Clown Show / $2.95 [See also Grove Press Modern Drama, John Lahr, ed., E633 / $5.95]

E577   GENET, JEAN / The Maids and Deathwatch: Two Plays / $3.95

E677   GRIFFITHS, TREVOR / The Comedians / $3.95

CRITICAL STUDIES

GROVE PRESS, INC., 196 West Houston St., New York, N.Y. 10014